The UN-AMERICAN President

Barack Obama

Thomas Brennan

For America

Foreword

Due to its industrial, military and economic strength The United States of America has had the ability to influence the governments and societies of the world more than any other country on earth for more than one hundred years. America's superior might in all of these arenas was clear from the late nineteenth century and then further demonstrated, in absolute terms, during World War II (1939-1945).

This unequivocal might has made the individual who holds the office of "The President" of the United States the most powerful and influential person in the world since that time.

Great power has attracted many men to the U.S. presidency who have made use of it: wielding a big stick and abusing, or at the very least making inappropriate use of, American might at many times in the country's history; as was the case with the presidents that led us into the First World War (World War I) and Viet Nam.

For the most part, however, America's presidents have shared a common belief in America. Most can be said to have truly loved their country. They believed in its founding principles, its freedoms, its opportunities and… its *exceptionalism*. And… they knew their country.

They knew that being the first successful democratic republic in the world at the time of its founding made America special. They knew that the fact that this republic had endured longer than any other had in history… made it special.

But now, for the first time in its history, America has elected what can aptly be called its first *"Un-American"* president.

This is not because he wasn't born here, (there are many who argue that he wasn't) but rather, because he is a president who, in both word and deed, has demonstrated that he does not share the views or beliefs of his predecessors or, for the most part, those of the American people.

Clearly, he does not share a belief in *"God and Country"* as do most Americans. This phrase has been an American mantra since the country's founding. It is also sadly clear that he has no conception, whatsoever, of what has made America great among the countries of the world: in either the past; or the present. And he most certainly does not believe in American exceptionalism.

This president has demonstrated time and again his disregard for the United States Constitution, the United States itself, and finally, for the American people. It should be noted that he took an oath to protect and preserve all of the above.

Whether or not he considers himself a citizen of the world: he has taken an oath on behalf of the American people and is therefore, responsible to them and to *their interests.*

Instead he has made it plain that he prefers socialism to capitalism, class preference to individual liberty, government control to free enterprise and world citizens' rights to American citizens' rights.

From his refusal to wear an American flag lapel pin during his election campaign to his refusal to secure America's borders and enforce even the Federal government's immigration laws; and then to also attack those that do; (i.e., the state of Arizona) this book documents some of the actions of this man to fundamentally change the country that he was elected to protect and preserve into a *psuedo-European* type of socialistic, government-controlled state; thereby earning him the distinction of truly being the country's first *Un-American President*. A president who considers himself to be *"above America."*

Contents

The Swindle

12

I. The Swindle

Barack Obama's statements that his election to the office of the President of the United States was improbable belies how little he actually knew of America and its people before his election and how glaringly wrong he has been about this country and its inhabitants in almost all respects.

And sadly, as wrong as Barack Obama was about the majority of Americans, so were fifty-five percent of them, wrong about him.

In the election, Barack Obama got fifty-six percent of the womens' vote, almost all of the youth vote (18-25), the vast majority of the hispanic vote and virtually all of the black vote.

These groups responded to his campaign's "Hope and Change" message without truly investigating what changes he had in mind.

In fact, the candidate Barack Obama was spared any kind of vetting process, whatsoever, and then was even treated with "kid gloves" by his political opponents. No one challenged his extraordinarily thin resume or his pitiful attendance and voting record in the United States Senate during his two years there.

He was in attendance but 150 days of his two years in that office and had more "present" (a non vote) votes than any other senator. Nor did anyone investigate what he actually did as a community organizer or, astoundingly, even what a community organizer was. For the record: in the case of Barack Obama, community organizing efforts involved getting money from the government and successful people and businesses to fund projects that would advantage minority groups and, in particular, African Americans. This involved legal pressure through threats of discrimination lawsuits against businesses and institutions, and associations with minority pressure groups such as ACORN, with which Barack Obama was directly involved, and for which, he personally provided legal services.

It was clear from the outset that Americans (and especially the American Press) were going to overlook the spotted past of this candidate and his very weak resume of accomplishments of any sort.

His college records were kept secret, the details of his activities as a community organizer were kept secret, his terrible Senate voting record was completely ignored, his scurrilous relationships with terrorists, racists and far left Marxist-socialists were completely ignored and were then even defended by America's left-leaning press.

This candidate said he was going to fundamentally change America without delineating what the changes would be and no one challenged any of this. Virtually nothing he said was challenged. Understandably, Barack Obama actually began to believe all the press and buzz about his brilliance even though he had said virtually nothing that ever really approached brilliance. However, with a teleprompter he was a practiced and talented speaker who could mesmerize his liberal sycophants. Unfortunately for all of us he caught a lot of independent voters in this spell as well.

What he *had deliberately done* had been to appeal to the emotions of the women, youth and minorities of America, knowing full well that among these groups pathos would be enough. There was no need for substance. Serious critics could easily be rendered impotent by veiled, if not outright, charges of racism, which America's biased and left-leaning press gladly provided for candidate Obama. So, challenges of any substance were non-existent.

More than ninety percent of America's journalists are registered democrats who promote a democratic party, "progressive" agenda and this candidate fit the bill as a leader for that agenda. Progressivism, by the way, is a metonym for leftist socialism.

What Barack Obama did not realize, however, is that he was also getting this special treatment for another reason. This reason *was his race*. Many, many white Americans voted for this man in spite of his shortcomings and past associations *because* he was black. Americans mistakenly believed that the election of an African-American president would be a way of finally putting to bed the incessant, one-sided charges of white American racism constantly levied by black "race industry" practitioners and their sycophants in America's biased press. In large part, white Americans felt that the country was ready for a black chief executive and they were happy to help elect him in the hope that it would be to the betterment of the country.

Barack Obama was clearly aware of the advantages his race was providing him *during the campaign*. The proof of this was his failure to abrogate the unfair and unfounded charges of racism that were leveled by democratic pundits and journalists against his opponents and critics.

Mere disagreement with candidate Obama was automatically labeled as racism by America's race-baiters both during and after the campaign. Obama should have renounced comments of this sort whenever they were falsely made: but he didn't.

There is such a thing as *a sin of omission.* If not bearing false witness against thy neighbor... how about: *allowing* false witness against thy neighbor...? Oh well, why split hairs?

Ironically, Obama did not consider that Americans would vote for him whether he was white or black. He didn't consider this because he believed America to be a racist country. He believed then, and astoundingly, still believes now, that this country is still an imperialist colonial empire, populated by white racists who immorally possess most of the wealth in the nation, which they procured through ill gotten means: on the backs of minorities.

So why was this election a swindle? It was a swindle because this candidate never *truthfully* divulged that he intended to forcibly redistribute the wealth and property of the American people. And he never divulged that he would take things even further by going on a campaign to instigate class warfare and divisiveness to accomplish these ends.

It was a swindle because the corps of American journalists not only failed to do their job (report the facts, truthfully and without bias) but; were actually *complicit* in a conspiracy to keep the truth about this candidate from the American people.

The most glaring example of this is the press' treatment of Barack and Michelle Obama's relationship with Jeremiah Wright, who is the pastor of the Trinity United Church of Christ on Chicago's south side.

For more than twenty years the two of them attended this church where religion is secondary to anti-white racist rants energized by deep-seated hatred of America and its white population: *born of fervid black on white racism.*

Not only did they attend Wright's church: They had him baptize their children. They had him marry them. And... they chose Jeremiah Wright to be their spiritual advisor!

During the campaign candidate Obama said that he had never really heard, or even listened to, any of the weekly racist rants of Jeremiah Wright in the twenty years he had attended Wright's church. Amazingly, our liberal American press represented this response to the public as *reasonable!* One has to work hard to keep a straight face when recalling members of the Democratic press stating that belonging to Wright's congregation was not significant. Not significant? Twenty years of hate America speeches?

Jeremiah Wright is the minister who cursed America the weekend following 911, ranting, "God Damn America," and blaming the U.S. for the actions of the terrorists.

So, this very Un-American minister preached for twenty years to this Un-American, soon to be, President and Un-American, soon to be, First Lady, but... this UN-American couple did not share the views of this vile bigot...? Please... Of course they did. His views reinforced their own views about racist, imperialist America. That's why they went to Wright's church. Michelle Obama herself stated in February of 2008 that for the first time in her adult life, she was proud of her country. This comment was made due to her husband's acceptance by America as a viable presidential candidate. Definitely a reference to what she had believed to be a racist America.

And... there are thousands of churches in Chicago... So why choose this one...?

A swindle is a deception: a fraudulent act.

The American people were indeed deceived: by the candidate himself, along with America's partisan press corps and American academia, all of whom perpetrated a fraud on the voters of the nation to serve their own political ends. This deception was built on lies, misrepresentations, slander against opponents and omissions of the truth. That's a swindle.

Liberals are remarkably Machiavellian... which relieves them of the burden of answering to a conscience.

The nefarious practices of the biased American media were not just restricted to covering for Obama; they also extended to slurs, distortions and unflattering portrayals of the Republican Vice Presidential candidate, Sarah Palin, whose credentials for the office were continually derided even though, by any measure, they exceeded those of presidential candidate, Barack Obama.

Here was a woman who, if a democrat, would have been celebrated as an American woman's success story. But, instead of being heralded for her considerable accomplishments, the left-leaning American media and leftist feminist organizations portrayed her as an unsophisticated, backwoods, redneck buffoon.

Virtually all of the country's journalists and news organizations conducted their interviews with candidate Palin as a means to ambush her with an endless barrage of "gotcha" questions designed to make her look uneducated, if not outright ignorant, and paint her as a dimwit who was totally incapable of holding high office. This negative campaign against Sarah Palin was relentless and devoid of honesty, and in that sense: it was immoral.

Finally, America was swindled, or at the very least short changed, by its Republican candidate for president. No attempt was made by Mr. McCain to challenge the character of Barack Obama, which was founded upon relationships with self-admitted terrorists, avowed socialists and racists. No challenge was made about Barack Obama's involvement with the notorious ACORN organization or of that mendacious organization's practices. No examination was demanded of candidate Obama's role and activities as a community organizer. No questions were raised as to why the Obamas would attend a church pastored by such an extreme racist. Instead

Mr. McCain remained silent and, in so doing, failed the American people.

There are times when a serious and comprehensive challenge to an individual's character and history must be mounted. One of those times is an election for the highest office in the land. Mr. McCain, in witnessing the absence of any vetting of candidate Obama by the press, should have undertaken the challenge himself on behalf of the American people; if for no other reason.

Since he did not, the country as a whole, was further deceived by Barack Obama. At least partially, this was a result of John McCain's and the Republican Party's (headed by John McCain) inaction and failure to mount a serious challenge to Obama's dubious background, his lack of veracity or his questionable character.

Whether McCain remained silent on these subjects due to some misplaced lofty notions about taking the high road, or because of some other reason known only to him, the result was that he was the last hope for the country to vet Barack Obama and get an honest look at this candidate.

Justified or not, to many Americans, John McCain and the Republican Party came off as either foolish or spineless rather than noble (with the exception of Governor Sarah Palin), who had wanted to challenge Barack Obama on all of the aforementioned issues, but was muzzled.

He Took An Oath...

II. *He Took An Oath...*

On January 20th 2009 Barack Hussein Obama was sworn into office as the newly elected President of the United States of America. In this ceremony he took the following oath:

"I, Barack Hussein Obama, do solemnly swear that I will faithfully execute the office of President of the United States, and will, to the best of my ability, preserve, protect, and defend the Constitution of the United States."

Definition of a constitution (From the Merriam Webster Dictionary)

The basic principles and laws of a nation, state, or social group that determine the powers and duties of government and guarantee certain rights to the people in it.

So, our constitution is the body of laws set down by our country's founders, (and thereafter, subsequent elected legislators), that govern our country and therefore its citizens. These laws also *guarantee* rights to America's citizens.

<u>Definition of preserve</u> (From the Merriam Webster Dictionary)

To maintain something in its existing state.

The President therefore, *by his own words*, is bound to uphold these laws (along with the rights they guarantee to American citizens).

It is also *implicit* in this oath that the person who holds the office of the President of the United States should act in America's interests and the interests of its citizens; *first and foremost.*

The president's duties of office listed in the Constitution (Article II; Sections 2 and 3) are as follows:

Section 2

The President shall be Commander in Chief of the Army and Navy of the United States, and of the Militia of the several States, when called into the actual Service of the United States; he may require the Opinion, in writing, of the principal Officer in each of the executive Departments, upon any subject relating to the Duties of their respective Offices, and he shall have Power to Grant Reprieves and Pardons for Offenses against the United States, except in Cases of Impeachment.

He shall have Power, by and with the Advice and Consent of the Senate, to make Treaties, provided two thirds of the Senators present concur; and he shall nominate, and by and with the Advice and Consent of the Senate, shall appoint Ambassadors, other public Ministers and Consuls, Judges of the supreme Court, and all other Officers of the United States, whose Appointments are not herein otherwise provided for, and which shall be established by Law: but the Congress may by Law vest the Appointment of such inferior Officers, as they think proper, in the President alone, in the Courts of Law, or in the Heads of Departments.

The President shall have Power to fill up all Vacancies that may happen during the Recess of the Senate, by granting Commissions which shall expire at the End of their next Session.

Section 3

He shall from time to time give to the Congress Information of the State of the Union, and recommend to their Consideration such Measures as he shall judged necessary and expedient; he may, on extraordinary Occasions, convene both Houses, or either of them, and in Case of Disagreement between them, with Respect to the Time of Adjournment, he may adjourn them to such Time as he shall think proper; he shall receive Ambassadors and other public Ministers; he shall take Care that the Laws be faithfully executed, and shall Commission all the Officers of the United States.

(A complete copy of the Constitution of The United States is contained in the last chapter of this book.)

By virtue of law and tradition, the roles of the President of the United States have evolved thusly:

Chief of State, chief executive, chief administrator, chief diplomat, the commander in chief of the armed forces and the chief legislator.

As chief of state the President is the head of the government. In the United States the President rules over the government, which is not true of chiefs of state in many other countries.

The President is also the country's chief executive and is vested with broad executive powers by the Constitution.

As the chief administrator, the President is in charge of the executive branch of the federal government. This branch employs more than 2.5 million civilians (and growing) and is the largest employer in the United States.

It is doubtful that this eventuality was envisioned by the authors of the original constitution.

The President is also the nation's chief diplomat and therefore, dictates and institutes America's foreign policy.

The Constitution makes the President the commander in chief of the armed forces, which, in addition to the army and navy mentioned in the Constitution, now includes other armed services and intelligence services such as the CIA, and the NSA as well as innumerable other agencies.

As the chief legislator of the country, the President can shape public policy. If he wishes he can submit his own legislation or request that Congress enact laws he believes are needed.

The powers of the presidency are broad, however, nowhere in the constitutional descriptions are listed powers or authority to re-distribute wealth or serve one class of citizens over another, nor is there authority to use taxpayers' funding to finance special endeavors, be they political, commercial or otherwise; as was done in the case of the unfolding Solyndra scandal, which was backed, if not engineered by, President Barack Obama and his administration.

First Order of Business

III. First Order of Business

In the summer and fall of 2008 banks and financial institutions were collapsing and panic was beginning to take hold in America. The domino effect of this collapse continued unabated well into early 2009, and of course, continues even now.

With this in mind, let's take a look at the first actions of the newly elected president in 2009.

Early in the year Barack Obama began traveling the globe and apologizing (inappropriately and without merit for the most part) for numerous actions, policies and indiscretions committed by the United States.

To date Barack Obama has apologized for America to billions of people across the globe in the Americas, Europe and the Muslim world.

The following are excerpts from speeches he made about the United States in just his first four months in office.

This apology was offered on January 27, 2009 during an interview with *Al Arabiya* (a major Muslim publication).

*"My job to the Muslim world is to communicate that the Americans are not your enemy. **We sometimes make mistakes. We have not been perfect.** But if you look at the track record, as you say, America was not born as a colonial power, and that the same respect and partnership that America had with the Muslim world as recently as 20 or 30 years ago, there's no reason why we can't restore that."*

This is paragraph from a speech made by President Obama to the French at the Rhenus Sports Arena, Strasbourg, France, April 3, 2009.

*"So we must be honest with ourselves. In recent years we've allowed our Alliance to drift. I know that there have been honest disagreements over policy, but we also know that there's something more that has crept into our relationship. **In America, there's a failure to appreciate Europe's leading role in the world. Instead of celebrating your dynamic union and seeking to partner with you to meet common challenges, there have been times where America has shown arrogance and been dismissive, even derisive."***

"Unfortunately, faced with an uncertain threat, our government made a series of hasty decisions. I believe that many of these decisions were motivated

by a sincere desire to protect the American people.
But I also believe that all too often our government
made decisions based on fear rather than foresight;
that all too often our government trimmed facts and
evidence to fit ideological predispositions. Instead of
strategically applying our power and our principles,
too often we set those principles aside as luxuries
that we could no longer afford. And during this
season of fear, too many of us, Democrats and
Republicans, politicians, journalists, and citizens
…fell silent.

President Obama, in an address to the Summit of the
Americas at the Hyatt Regency, Port of Spain,
Trinidad and Tobago, April 17, 2009.

"All of us must now renew the common stake that we
have in one another. ***I know that promises of***
partnership have gone unfulfilled in the past, and
that trust has to be earned over time. While the
United States has done much to promote peace and
prosperity in the hemisphere, we have at times been
disengaged, and at times we sought to dictate our
terms. *But I pledge to you that we seek an equal*
partnership. There is no senior partner and junior
partner in our relations; there is simply engagement
based on mutual respect and common interests and
shared values. So I'm here to launch a new chapter of

engagement that will be sustained throughout my administration.

The United States will be willing to acknowledge past errors where those errors have been made."

And on April 6th 2009 Obama made this statement to the Turkish Parliament at Ankara, Turkey.

"Every challenge that we face is more easily met if we tend to our own democratic foundation. This work is never over. **That's why, in the United States, we recently ordered the prison at Guantanamo Bay closed. That's why we prohibited, without exception or equivocation, the use of torture. All of us have to change. And sometimes change is hard.**

Another issue that confronts all democracies as they move to the future is how we deal with the past. The United States is still working through some of our own darker periods in our history *Facing the Washington Monument that I spoke of is a memorial of Abraham Lincoln, the man who freed those who were enslaved even after Washington led our Revolution.* **Our country still struggles with the legacies of slavery and segregation, the past treatment of Native Americans.**

*Human endeavor is by its nature imperfect. History is often tragic, **but unresolved, it can be a heavy weight. Each country must work through its past.** And reckoning with the past can help us seize a better future.*"

The following is an opinion editorial piece from President Obama on April 16th 2009 about our neighboring countries in Central and South America

*"**Too often, the United States has not pursued and sustained engagement with our neighbors.** We have **been too easily distracted by other priorities,** and have failed to see that our own progress is tied directly to progress throughout the Americas. My Administration is committed to the promise of a new day. We will renew and sustain a broader partnership between the United States and the hemisphere on behalf of our common prosperity and our common security."*

Below are remarks made by the President to CIA employees at CIA headquarters in Langley, Virginia on April 20th 2009. This address was made after the administration's decision to release details about America's enhanced interrogation techniques used against terror suspects.

"So don't be discouraged by what's happened in the last few weeks. Don't be discouraged that we have to acknowledge potentially we've made some mistakes. That's how we learn. But the fact that we are willing to acknowledge them and then move forward, that is precisely why I am proud to be President of the United States, and that's why you should be proud to be members of the CIA."

There were more apologetic speeches to follow and one in particular, where President Obama addressed an audience of thousands of prominent Muslims in Cairo, **in which he blamed heightened tensions between Muslims and the U.S. on American colonialism, which he said "deprived" Muslims of opportunities.** Making statements such as these offers a degree of legitimacy to the monstrous actions of Islamic terrorists in America and throughout the world.

With respect to these "apology tours," the greatest humiliation to be visited upon the United States by this president, thankfully, didn't happen. But, Obama had planned to fly to Japan in the fall of 2009 and visit both Hiroshima and Nagasaki for the purposes of apologizing, on behalf of the U.S., for dropping atomic bombs on these two cities in World War II. Barack Obama's intention to make apologies for these bombings reveals an astonishing, if not jarring, lack of knowledge of the history of that war and a complete ignorance of the desperation of that hour. Fortunately, the Japanese themselves nixed Obama's plans to make these apologies and thus saved the United States from this additional gross indignity.

Why President Obama felt it necessary to make these apologetic statements and conciliatory admissions is a mystery, but one can only assume that they reflect his actual beliefs about the United States of America.

Certainly they should not have been made on behalf of the American people because the majority of Americans did not share these views at the time he made these statements, nor do they now.

A mere eight years after 911: it was not the time to criticize interrogation techniques employed by the U.S. when dealing with Islamic terrorists. Likewise, nor were the conditions at Guantanamo of paramount consideration in light of the monstrous acts of terror committed against innocent American civilians in New York, Washington and in the skies over Shanksville, Pennsylvania on 911.

Many of Obama's comments were veiled attempts designed to mitigate foreign resentments over

America's military actions and involvements (including those of the C.I.A.) throughout the world.

It might then have been appropriate to cite the fact that America's military has been responsible for delivering freedom from oppression and the gift of democracy to more "peoples" than any other government, organization or institution *in the entire history of the world.* Perhaps more emphasis of the positive may have been wise.

The comments in these addresses would not, in and of themselves, have been controversial except that they were unbalanced. The President did not call upon the audiences he was addressing to examine any of the injustices or iniquities in their own countries. For example: Why did he not take the occasion in Cairo to bring up the outright criminal treatment of women in Muslim countries; or the intolerance towards any other religions in the majority of these countries; or the lack of democratic governments in the majority of Muslim run countries?

Why did he not bring up the glaring *absence of people of color* as leaders in European governments; or the corrupt governments throughout Central and South America; or the murder, violence and even genocides exacted against entire populations by African regimes, and so on...?

The point is that he, as a major world leader, should not be pandering to other countries by presenting criticisms of the United States without offering a balanced view; without so much as a mention of the very widely practiced, and even routine, offenses against freedom and civil rights found all over the world.

It is important to keep in mind that Barack Obama embarked upon these now infamous *"apology tours"* immediately after taking office. Hence, they were undoubtedly planned as a *first order of business* for his new administration.

In fairness to the President, some of these addresses would more correctly be called appeasement speeches rather than apologies. However, whatever they are called, it is obvious that these addresses were ill timed, one-sided, unnecessary and, at the very least, not flattering to the country or citizens that had just elected him as their president.

All of this aside, the paramount issue really is: **Why** did Barack Obama feel it necessary to make these global conciliations so early on after taking office?

"Americanism"

versus

Socialism

IV. Americanism vs. Socialism

What is Americanism? Americanism is the uniquely free and very much capitalist, societal system, which has prospered Americans more than any other people in the history of the world for the two hundred years of the country's existence: the principal precepts of which have been minimal government interference and control upon the lives of America's citizens.

Said another way: *Liberty...*

Socialism is, for all intents and purposes, its opposite. Said another way: *Big Brother...*

Leftists, liberals, socialists and progressives are all different names for the same people: all cut from the same cloth. They all believe in big government and that government, and of course, *they themselves*, know what's best for the people.

Americanism is built upon the belief that *the people* know what's best for the people.

Just to be sure that the differences are understood concise definitions of both capitalism and socialism follow.

Capitalism is an economic and political system in which the country's trade, production and sales are controlled by private owners and enterprises as opposed to government ownership.

Socialism is an economic and political system whereby the government owns and maintains control over the trade, production and commerce of a nation or state.

However, in practice, socialism is a system whose controls go far beyond the areas of commerce and enterprise; also exerting controls over virtually everything of import in a society, including: education, health-care, housing and all areas of industry.

This has been seen to be true in all of the socialist countries of the world including China: where its socialist government even dictated the gender and number of children the Chinese were allowed to have per family.

Communism is a political and societal system derived from Karl Marx, encouraging class warfare and leading to a society in which all property is publicly owned and each person works and is paid according to their abilities and needs.

The definition of communism is included here due to it being the progenitor and orthodox form of socialism.

America has been the world's greatest breeding ground for free enterprise and invention for the last two hundred years... *because of its free capitalist system.* America's free, capitalist society has been what has attracted so many millions of immigrants to migrate to its shores to build futures for themselves and their families over this period of time.

But today, the opportunities that America's free capitalist system has traditionally offered to its citizens are in jeopardy. These opportunities are in jeopardy because the freedoms that foster them are being taken away by one of America's two major political parties: which has socialism at the heart of its doctrine.

America has now been commandeered by socialists to a degree that it has here-to-fore never experienced. Not because there have not been socialist presidents or congresses before; there have. Socialists have infiltrated the White House and halls of Congress in great numbers since the early nineteen hundreds. But now these legislators have the press and the educators of academia as allies in league with them. And there is a concerted effort on the part of all of them to *"fundamentally change America."* Sound familiar?

To accomplish their ends the socialists and progressives have encouraged, and even actively orchestrated, class warfare, racism and open immigration. Socialists and progressives are also the inventors of *political correctness*, which they employ against their detractors indiscriminately: using it as an intimidation technique.

Under the current president, class warfare is used routinely to achieve political ends. But, even before Obama's election, the Democratic Party was using this tactic as well as that of class favoritism; one instance of which was largely responsible for the massive housing industry debacle, which precipitated the economic crash of 2008.

In 1977 the Democratic Party, led by Jimmy Carter, in typical socialistic fashion, sponsored legislation (The Community Redevelopment Act) to relax standards on lending to extend mortgages to people in low to moderate income areas; particularly the inner cities. This policy would make home ownership possible for large segments of low income and minority populations throughout the U.S.

Then, in the 1990's the Clinton administration *forced* further relaxation *(lowering)* of the lending standards directed at these groups. Clinton went so far as to have his Attorney General (Janet Reno) and other federal agencies notify the banks and lending institutions that they would be prosecuted for discriminatory practices and face the bad publicity associated with those prosecutions if they did not lower their lending standards and extend mortgage loans to people who would otherwise not qualify for them.

The N.Y.Times reported that, as a result, the growth of home ownership in the United States jumped dramatically during the Clinton administration. In 1993 it was 63 percent; by the end of the Clinton administration it was 68 percent *(a gigantic leap for such a short period of time)*. The growth in the Bush administration was about 1 percent.

The N.Y. Times also reported in 1999 that Fannie Mae and Freddie Mac (government backed mortgage lending institutions) were *under pressure* from the Clinton administration to increase their lending to minorities and low-income home buyers: a policy that necessarily entailed higher risks.

As a consequence of this government meddling and pressure additional millions of people were not held to prudent lending standards and were given home loans regardless of their ability to make the payments on these mortgages. The potential for disaster should have been obvious to all concerned at that point, but there were few voices of dissent to the risky lending. President Bush, however, was one of them. He cautioned against the further extension of these lax lending policies and warned of the potential for a financial meltdown in the housing and banking sectors of the economy. His warnings were ignored and he was assured by the congressional committee in charge of the regulation of these loans (specifically Barney Frank, D –Massachusetts - Chairman of the House Financial Services Committee) that the lending institutions were sound and that the housing market was in good shape and, in fact, that the programs were working as they should.

So, these government sponsored, and indeed, forced lending policies were building a mountain of red ink for the lenders *and the tsunami had yet to hit the shore!*

The people forgotten in all of this, of course, were the taxpayers and also, the stock-holders of the lending institutions and banks, who would eventually have to bite the bullet and suffer the losses on behalf of those who did not pay their mortgages. The stockholders mentioned here were not large Wall Street investors: for the most part they were average everyday people with large portions of their personal savings invested in these bank stocks.

We all know what happened next.

Prior to the collapse Mike Stathis (a prominent financial investment analyst) warned about the risks of Fannie Mae triggering the financial crisis in America's Financial Apocalypse. *"With close to $2 trillion in debt between Freddie Mac and Fannie Mae alone, as well as several trillion held by commercial banks, failure of just one GSE (government sponsored enterprise) or related entity could create a huge disaster that would easily eclipse the Savings & Loan Crisis of the late 1980s. This would certainly devastate the stock, bond and real estate markets. Most likely, there would also be an even bigger mess in the derivatives market, leading to a global sell-off in the capital markets. Not only would investors get crushed, but taxpayers would have to bail them out since the GSEs are backed by the government. Everyone would feel the effects"*.

If only these warnings had been heeded, but Barney Frank stated the following to the Boston Globe,

"The private sector got us into this mess. The government has to get us out of it."

That's Barney Frank's take. And it is a far cry from the truth. The Congress had *great* culpability in this fiasco. The Democratic Party had engineered it.

But according to Frank the financial crisis was the spawn of the free market run amok, with the political class guilty *only* of failing to rein the capitalists in. The Wall Street meltdown was caused by "bad decisions that were made by people in the private sector," Frank said; the country is in dire straits today "thanks to a conservative philosophy that says the market knows best." And that philosophy goes "back to Ronald Reagan, when at his inauguration he said, 'Government is not the answer to our problems; government is the problem.' " *This quote by Frank is incorrect.*

That aside, this convoluted version of the facts is clearly designed to deflect criticism from him, and is all too typical of socialist adherents, who rarely accept culpability for their actions and the failures of their programs, which they force upon the public.

The housing industry represents such a large part of the economy of the United States that its fall would necessarily have a ripple effect upon the entire economy, affecting retail sales and services to a staggering degree. But the biggest and by far most detrimental effect was the huge number of foreclosures it caused throughout the country, the defaulted mortgages of which, both the issuing banks and the government (who had guaranteed the bad loans) had to make good on. The government, of course, has no money, so the taxpayers were left to foot the bill.

The financial catastrophe described here is the result of but one of the socialist initiatives that have gone wrong and had disastrous unintended consequences in the history of the United States. This socialistic program was recent but one does not have to look back far to see other examples: Franklin Roosevelt's "New Deal" in the 1930's, which prolonged the Great Depression it was intended to end: and also, Lyndon Johnson's "Great Society" programs in the 1960's, which were designed to end poverty in the United States, but which, in actuality, created an enormous welfare state and huge debts to pay for it. By the way, it didn't end poverty.

Socialism is always sold as an ideal political and economic system that promises equal prosperity for everyone. Equality maybe: but not prosperity.

The truth is that socialism will provide a meager existence for everyone if taken to its logical extreme. History has demonstrated this unassailably in the example of the former Soviet Union.

It should be mentioned that Republicans, too, bear immense responsibility for the financial crisis that overtook the United States in 2008. And this crisis involved more than the housing and real estate markets to be sure, but the point made here is that in the case of the housing and real estate debacles, *which were the agents of impetus that started the slide of everything else*, it was the socialistic policies of the federal government that set the stage for the eventual outcome.

While many causes for the financial crisis have been suggested, the United States Senate, issuing the Levin–Coburn Report found "that the crisis was not a natural disaster, but the result of high risk, complex financial products; undisclosed conflicts of interest; and the failure of regulators, the credit rating agencies, and the market itself to rein in the excesses of Wall Street." It was further argued that credit rating agencies and investors failed to accurately price (assess) the risk involved *with mortgage related financial products* and that *governments* did not adjust their regulatory practices to address 21st-century financial markets.

This is sugar-coating it, which obfuscates the truth… the simple fact of the matter is that the credit rating agencies and lenders were *forced by the government* to disregard their own prudent standards and make the bad loans to people who were not creditworthy; it was not their idea; which makes the point: If Americanism had been left to its own devices the banks and mortgage lenders would have used their normal credit standards and these millions of bad loans, amounting to trillions of dollars, would never have been made in the first place.

This is not to say that there isn't a need for government legislation, but rather, that when that legislation is designed for the purposes of social and financial engineering to advantage one group by disadvantaging other groups (in this case the middle class and all American taxpayers) it is discrimination on a grand scale and absolutely adverse to the Constitution. And when the government then deliberately interferes with private enterprise, compelling it to conform to such discriminatory regulations in order to achieve those ends: the government has clearly exceeded its purview.

Integral to Americanism is the maxim of less government control and interference with the citizenry. Socialism is therefore antithetical to Americanism and President Barack Obama is one of its most enthusiastic and aggressive proponents.

Barack Obama:

Socialist

V. Barack Obama: Socialist

When presidential candidate Newt Gingrich was asked if Barack Obama was a socialist his answer was succinct, "Of course he is."

During his famous verbal exchange with "Joe the plumber" during his election campaign Barack Obama as much as admitted so by stating that it would be good to take some of the plumber's income and spread it around. Much was made of Obama's statements to the plumber and the candidate quickly learned to subdue his comments concerning the re-distribution of wealth, which of course, is a hallmark of socialism.

Whatever one thinks of President Obama, it is indisputable, by virtue of his own words and actions, that he is indeed, a committed socialist, and that his plan to fundamentally change America is indeed, a plan to change America's form of society from capitalist to socialist, with much greater government involvement and control over major sectors of the economy and society. This is evidenced by his initiatives for government control over healthcare and energy, in particular.

Since taking office, the President's socialist, big government fingerprints can be seen on virtually all of his initiatives, which almost always call for the forced transfer of wealth from one group to another, or the levy of additional taxes on specific groups or industries, to achieve his objectives.

These transfers of wealth are not just restricted to income taxes on individuals or corporations, but will also be accomplished by outlawing (through legislation) existing businesses, and, the levying of unreasonable taxes on the goods or services provided by certain businesses for the purposes of forcing consumers to use the alternatives he has ordained for the nation. These are the action plans of Barack Obama. We know this - because he said so.

Obama stated prior to his election that his energy plan called for the elimination of fossil fuels such as coal and oil and for their replacement with green sources of energy. His plan to accomplish this was to price the fossil fuels out of the market by placing *such excessive taxes on them* that their continued use would be impractical for all but the rich. He has as much as said that he wants to bankrupt the coal industry in this manner.

Incredibly, even now, with economic conditions being what they are, he is continuing with this agenda regardless of the economy and without regard for the fact that increased energy costs at this juncture could be the straw that breaks the camel's back for most American families.

And though his chances of passing legislation that would include any additional taxes on anything right now are not very likely, Obama is still pushing the alternative energy sources whether practical or not, and, whether wasteful (of tax dollars) or not.

Solyndra is a recent example and it is just the tip of the iceberg. In this case Solyndra (a solar panel manufacturer) was given a $528,000,000 government loan (that's five-hundred and twenty-eight million tax dollars) in spite of the fact that the Obama administration was told *in advance* that Solyndra was financially unsound, insolvent, had little chance of becoming solvent and would indeed, go bankrupt in short order. The President went ahead with the loan anyway, wasting a half *billion* dollars of Americans' money. A half billion dollars is a big chunk of the deficit that we have to erase. The President then added insult to injury by responding in a cavalier manner about the loss of the half billion dollars in an ABC News interview with George Stephanopolous.

It should be noted here that it has been reported by Bill O'Reilly of Fox News that both Larry Summers (Head of The United States National Economic Council, appointed by President Barack Obama) and Timothy Geitner (Secretary of the Treasury, appointed by President Obama) both felt that an investment in Solyndra was a bad deal that was extremely risky and consequently should not be made.

Obama has been touting Spain as a model of a country that was successfully transitioning to green energy production from fossil fuels. Unfortunately, it is now common knowledge that Spain has failed in this effort and that the country's attempt to make this transition has all but collapsed its economy.

Spain's own government analysts reported these results (to our Congress), pointing out that for every green job created two and one half existing jobs were lost and that energy costs for consumers increased dramatically. Barack Obama and the Democratic members of Congress then *rejected Spain's findings* and consequently, Obama's agenda to spend the billions on green energy continues: full steam ahead.

Although Obama did not originally sponsor the lightbulb bill that bans incandescent bulbs in favor of the new mercury tainted energy saver bulbs, he is nonetheless fully behind the enforcement of this law, and this is despite the fact that it is already costing Americans jobs.

GE (General Electric), a major manufacturer of the new bulbs recently closed one of its plants in Virginia that had been making incandescent bulbs because it will now be making the new mercury filled bulbs instead – in Mexico. Regardless of the unpopularity of this new law and the new bulb's safety issues, the Democrats and Barack Obama have blocked Republican attempts in the House to redress the issue.

And the list goes on:

The Department of Labor has given untold millions of dollars to colleges and schools for training for green jobs: ***that do not exist!***

After getting a 150 billion dollar bailout, GM was given a $250 million dollar grant for the Volt electric car, another $150 million for a Korean company to build parts of the car and the government now pays buyers of the Volt a $7,500 rebate for purchasing the car. The result: GM has sold 4,000 Volt vehicles.

Tessla Motors received $500 million to build its electric car and its buyers also receive the $7,500 rebate: *whether they need it or not*. Tessla's electric vehicles are upscale cars with hefty price tags (As of this writing the lowest priced models started at $55,000).

A Michigan solar shingle manufacturing company that Obama touted as an example of a successful green energy company received a low interest loan from the government, which helped the company immensely according to the company's owners, but that's not all that is turning this company into a success story. What is, is the fact that, in addition to the low interest loan, the government also pays the consumers (with tax money) who buy this company's products with cash rebates and credits that can make them thousands of dollars a month *in profit!* It certainly won't be all that hard for green companies to succeed if they get deals wherein the government (the taxpayer) pays their customers thousands of dollars a month to buy their products. Even if the blatantly unfair favoritism in all of these programs is left un-addressed: policies such as this are invalid in their own right, as they give no honest measure of the consumers' desire for a commodity or product. Especially when the rebates given not only reimburse the cost of the product, but also deliver a profit.

Barack Obama plans to spend a whopping $150 billion of Americans money to invest in green energy companies. In spite of the fact that the investigation of the Solyndra fiasco is still ongoing and that the reasons for this monumentally bad decision have yet to be determined, the Obama administration already has an additional five billion dollars approved to be given to other solar companies immediately; with billions more to come after that. Caution or prudence of any sort is apparently being thrown to the wind when it comes to green energy: *no pun intended.*

Barack Obama has been extraordinarily bold since taking office. Of course he could afford to be since he was elected by a majority of the voters and his party had also gained complete control of Congress by winning majorities in both the Senate and the House of Representatives. Said another way: he owned the government.

This situation provided the "Perfect Storm" for a president to bull through controversial legislation. It was the opportune time to force socialized medicine on the country and pass the Democratic Party's Health Care Bill.

However, this bill was so controversial and so sweeping in scope that even with Democratic Party threats to withdraw reelection support and funding for Democratic politicians who did not vote for the bill, some Democrats still withheld support. In the end it was passed by only seven votes in the House. Clearly a house divided and not a sweeping mandate by any means: particularly in view of the Democratic Party's strong arm tactics practiced on its own members.

This health care bill may be noble in its intent, but as with most Obama plans it is remarkably deficient when it comes to its design and practicality. This is not at all surprising considering the fact that most of the congressmen and congresswomen who voted this bill into law had not even read it in its entirety; the most notable being Nancy Pelosi, Majority Leader of the House of Representatives and leader of the Democratic Party, second in command only to Barack Obama himself. She hadn't even read the bill even though its passage into law would affect every single American citizen. Astounding… but true.

Putting aside the fact that this health care bill may be un-Constitutional and is likely to be found so by virtue of the fact that it forces all American citizens to purchase government dictated insurance plans whether those individuals wish to or not, it is an enormous program that will be enormously difficult for the states to implement and enforce. Many governors have already stated that its implementation would bankrupt their states.

The Supreme Court will hear challenges to the new law and decide on the constitutionality of parts of this legislation early this year (2012).

Proponents of the Health Care Bill are jubilant in their belief that it will provide health care for everyone. However, subsequent examination of the law has proven this to be untrue.

Both before and after the bill's passage, countless physicians have testified that the bill will necessarily result in lower quality medical care for patients overall. *The effect socialized medicine has had in Europe.*

And in general, detractors feel that the health care law will negatively affect the quality of their own healthcare in order for the medical industry to adequately provide care for those who cannot provide it for themselves.

This set of new health care laws is so gargantuan that it took many employers the better part of a year to calculate the costs it would impose upon them to provide health insurance as a benefit for their employees. Likewise, numerous employers have also stated that it will put them under additional financial pressure and limit the amount of new hiring that they will be able to do after its enactment.

Whether pro or con and valid or not, these arguments are of no consequence because these will not be the arguments before the Supreme Court. The arguments before the court will revolve around the rights of individuals' and states rights: *i.e.*, *Does the Federal Government have the right to compel citizens and states to comply with the mandates contained in the Health Care Bill?*

And: *Does the Federal Government have the right to force individuals to purchase products or services according to its dictates?*

Advocates of Barack Obama's health care bill argue that the Federal Government of the United States is granted these powers in the *Commerce Clause* of the Constitution.

The clause (Article I, Section 8, Clause 3) states that the United States Congress shall have power to regulate commerce with foreign nations, and among the several states, and with the Indian Tribes".

Progressive-socialists and Democratic Party members *(the majority of whom are progressive-socialists)* clearly fall on the side of the federal mandates.

By and large, the majority of the country's educators *(most of whom are also progressive-socialists)* support the Federal Government's right to impose mandates as well.

However, the majority of Americans are opposed to this bill. They believe in the rights of the individual. They believe in the Constitution. And they believe in *Americanism*. Most Americans still think that they are lucky to be in America and most of those who immigrate here *legally*, think that too.

Being an American is apparently not something that President Obama seemingly places much value on. Nor does he have an appreciation for Americanism as a socio-economic system.

Instead Barack Obama is moving us very fast to a European socio-economic model. This is in the face of the continuing failures of European countries and the socialist systems they've adopted. In spite of the Europeans' inability to do so in their own countries, Barack Obama believes that the Federal Government *can control* the nation's economy.

Even worse, he believes that the Federal Government *should control* the nation's economy.

Through his love of federal programs that are designed to control all facets of our society the President has demonstrated, in no uncertain terms, that it is his aspiration to transform the United States of America into a socialist republic and that he, indeed, intends to do just that.

And, worse yet: Barack Obama believes that the Federal Government *has the right* to control the nation's economy, which is absolutely adverse to the United States Constitution and therefore antithetical to Americanism.

In light of the fact that Obama has been acclaimed as a constitutional scholar it is astonishing that he fails to grasp that the very purpose of the Constitution of the United States from the outset... *was to limit the power of the federal government.*

So, either he doesn't know this, or he doesn't believe in this. In either case: neither his ignorance nor his beliefs relieve him of the accountability for his actions, which are to say the least, UN-American.

Barack Obama even put the country's economic crisis (*which he himself called the greatest economic crisis since the Great Depression*) on the back burner, in order to instead martial his forces to push his socialized health care plan on America. He literally had to be forced by his own party to prioritize the economic crisis.

It should now be crystal clear that Barack Obama is a devout progressive democrat and socialist who believes that the government knows best what America's policies ought to be and will use any measures at his disposal to enact his initiatives regardless of individuals' rights or the economic consequences to the country.

He of course believes this, so long as *he is the head of that government.* At this point it has become self-evident that the will of the people is not a part of his decision-making process: if that will disagrees with *his agenda*.

The damage to this republic caused by this one man is almost incalculable but, ironically, can be summed up in one sentence: *He pulled off a coup... literally.*

Barack Obama has done more to advance socialism in this country than any other president in American history with the possible exception of Franklin Roosevelt.

And just as Roosevelt's programs prolonged the Great Depression, likewise Barack Obama's are prolonging a recovery from America's present recession. If anything, his programs have hurt the economy and very much worsened the recession.

But, of greater importance, is that this president is doing very considerable damage to American society with huge programs that are sweeping in scope that will, in turn, have enormous and far reaching effects on the country. Detrimental effects.

And... they will not be just economic.

Driving the Economy

Turn Left!

VI. Driving The Economy: *Turn Left!*

Although the economic policies of Barack Obama cannot all be said to have been inherently socialist, neither have any been guided by capitalist principles: one of those being less government control.

His decisions are always driven by leftist, socialist dogma. Always there is the reluctance to relinquish control and an urgency to seize it when an opportunity presents itself. Always there is government intervention and regulation. And always, will the interests of a class, or cause, take precedence over rational economic policy. That's dogma.

Barack Obama can easily turn the economy around if he so chooses. He can do it in a mere month. But he won't. He won't because to do that he would have to loose the energy production engines of America and allow domestic development and production of natural gas and oil.

The United States has huge reservoirs of natural gas and oil; including shale oil. These reservoirs exist in the contiguous 48 states as well as Alaska. It is now estimated that North Dakota's reserves alone, exceed those of Mid-eastern countries.

Elimination of the regulations that prohibit domestic production of these natural resources would instantly kick-start the economy and *create millions of jobs.* Good paying jobs. Overnight.

Today, oil drilling is not the threat to the environment it was in the 1970s, and particularly so when drilling on land. It is common sense that controlling an accidental spill on land would be logistically much easier than controlling one 500 feet below the ocean. Also, drilling and delivery safety measures have improved dramatically since the time that the prohibitions against domestic production were imposed. The increased drilling and production being done safely by other countries is proof of this.

But, Obama and the Democrats won't even entertain the relaxation of the regulations prohibiting drilling and domestic development: even with the knowledge that it would dramatically improve the economy, reduce unemployment and bring down the deficit. That's dogma.

We saw this irrationality in action right in front of our eyes when Barack Obama immediately imposed a moratorium prohibiting any drilling in the Gulf of Mexico after the BP oil spill. A moratorium that cost upwards of thirty thousand American jobs by the most conservative of estimates.

And then, in an act of unmitigated audacity, Obama struck a deal with Brazil (in which he gave them 5 billion U.S. dollars to finance drilling – *their drilling*) for the United States to import oil - *their oil.* Upon the consummation of this deal the President even went so far as to say *publicly* that the United States wished to be Brazil's best customer!

Putting all this aside, Barack Obama has failed to do things within his purview that would lower the burden on America's businesses and thus, help the economy.

He could be pressing to bring tax rates for American corporations down to a level that is on par with those of other countries. America's tax rates for corporations are higher than those of all but a few other countries.

And if he did nothing else, Obama could release the strangle hold that federal agencies and their excessive regulations have on American businesses. This would lower the business's operating costs and give them the ability to do at least some additional hiring, or perhaps even, to expand into new areas.

Instead, he pushes forward with more regulation on existing businesses and industries while he spends taxpayers' money on unsuccessful green-industry programs that are not practical and premature in their technology.

Barack Obama and his policies are responsible for increasing the federal deficit by 4.2 Trillion dollars (nearly doubling that of George Bush's deficit in just his three years in office as opposed to Bush's eight), increasing unemployment to over 9% (with virtually no jobs created), over two million mortgage foreclosures (and counting) and fifty percent higher gasoline prices. Obama spent nearly a trillion dollars with this result. This is beyond bad: it's abysmal.

President Obama has indisputably demonstrated that he has absolutely no understanding, whatsoever, of how a free market economy works, or should work; and that he is devoid of any ideas as to how to stimulate *any* economy; let alone one this large.

He is, however, very adept at stimulating growth in the government that he presides over and equally adroit when it comes to spending taxpayers' money. The Federal Government is now thirty percent (30%) larger than it was just four years ago.

The percent of the government's overall spending to Gross Domestic Productivity is now approaching the levels seen during World War II; the highest in the country's history and unsustainable.

But with size comes greater productivity... right? Under Obama's stewardship federal agencies are issuing new regulations that are strangling businesses in all industries and on all levels; and they're doing this at an unprecedented rate. According to nationally syndicated radio host and constitutional scholar, Mark Levin, the federal government is issuing sixty-five to seventy thousand new regulations **every year.** That's 65,000 to 70,000 new laws that business owners and people have to comply with – each year!

The President of the United States, as the country's chief executive, is the one person who can reverse this situation and take these excessive regulations off the backs of America's businesses. He is in charge of every one of these out of control agencies. But, instead of reigning them in and preventing them from hampering businesses he uses these agencies as weapons against companies that do not comply with both his, and the liberal left's, agenda.

A stellar example of this is the recent action of the Obama Administration when it asked the National Labor Relations Board (a federal government agency created to oversee relations between unions and employers) to file suit in court to prevent Boeing from opening and operating a new plant in the state of South Carolina. This plant would create 3,800 jobs and these would be high paying, permanent jobs. But, these would also be non-union jobs, so the Obama administration wants to force Boeing to close the plant and bring these operations back to Washington State where the plant had originally been planned to open. There, of course, the plant would have union employees.

The National Labor Relations Board is made up of a five-member panel that has been controlled by the Democratic Party since 2009, so Barack Obama knew full well that he could count on the board's support to file the lawsuit against Boeing.

In terms of the economy, Americans are not likely to see any relief in the near future since, on top of what has already been mentioned, the Health Care Bill is expected to have an adverse effect; increasing costs for businesses and employers, which will in turn inhibit hiring and new job creation.

And in addition, for the most part, the programs advocated by the President thus far call for additional taxation to close the deficit gap and also contain additional regulations that place further burdens on businesses that will impede their growth.

On the bright side: there are one hundred and forty thousand new jobs. Government jobs...

Ignorance

and

Arrogance

VII. Ignorance *and* Arrogance

When witnessing some of the things Barack Obama has said and done, it's hard at first glance to discern if they were done out of ignorance or arrogance.

From early on these blunders ranged from being monumental flaws in judgment to just utterly stupid gaffs, as in the case of Barack Obama's reaction towards the Cambridge, Massachusetts police in the Skip Gates incident, which resulted in the ridiculous "beer summit" Obama hosted for the parties who were initially involved.

The Skip Gates Incident

In this incident Harvard professor Skip Gates was arrested when the police responded to a possible attempted burglary at the professor's home. Gates appeared to be trying to jimmy the door of the house. When the police demanded that he show identification to prove that he lived at the residence Professor Gates became belligerent, abusive and then, as the police attempted to exit the premises, he followed them, hurling insults at the officers and accusing them of racism. Clearly, the professor was in the wrong and overreacted in the extreme.

An incident this minor does not normally warrant a response from a sitting president of the United States.

However, Skip Gates is a friend of Barack Obama's and so the President appeared on national television with the unbelievable response that the police behaved "stupidly" in this incident.

Apparently, President Obama hadn't apprised himself of the facts of the case before making his prejudicial and incendiary statement. Incendiary because Gates was charging the police with racism towards him *because he was black* and therefore, Obama's baseless comments just added fuel to this fire. The poor judgment shown by the President here is almost unfathomable.

Here was an otherwise small incident made bigger by Obama's inappropriate and uninformed comments. He publicly, and unjustly, maligned the police and the officer involved.

Rather than make an apology to the police the President staged the preposterous and juvenile beer summit in the Rose Garden to diffuse the situation. A situation he himself created; which would not have been a situation at all but for his prejudicial and inappropriate comments made on national TV.

It is then quite reasonable to question whether the beer summit itself was actually staged for the purposes of damage control: to prevent the Gate's episode from turning into a full-blown racial incident and also; to divert attention from President Barack Obama's biased and foolish comments.

There were people who behaved stupidly in this incident, the President himself being one of them, but it was not the police officer. Putting all other considerations aside one has to question the "wisdom" of this purportedly intelligent man (the President).

The Apology Tours

The heart of socialism is Europe and Barack Obama apparently views himself as a global leader: and in the European tradition, a socialist leader.

When one considers this possibility it is then possible to understand his motivations for making his now infamous apology tours right after taking office and his comments to Muslims, in particular.

After all, a global leader would necessarily be required to rise above nationalism and resolve international disputes by using the enlightened understanding that comes with the larger view that *only a true globalist would possess.*

If this was his intention, which is how it came off, it might have been prudent to add some historical context and at least a modicum of wisdom to his repertoire.

The speeches delivered during these tours have already been cited in this book because they were unbalanced, invalid and did not, by any means, serve America's interests, however, there are additional things to be considered concerning them.

The motivations behind these addresses appear to be due to either, ignorance, arrogance, or both. They certainly were arrogant in the sense that Barack Obama was being critical of America's foreign policies (many of which he has now decided to continue with) without giving a true account of the reasons for their deployment in the first place. His one sided criticisms of the United States demonstrated that he did not have a grasp of all of the dynamics that shaped America's policies. Therefore his criticisms were based solely on his own biased and less than favorable view of the United States. That's ignorance... Or is it arrogance?

The Health Care Summit

Feb 25, 2010. Anyone who witnessed the televised portions of this summit had to be taken back by the unfiltered arrogance displayed by Barack Obama during this meeting, when in a disagreement with John McCain the President snapped at him saying, "The election is over, John," and then smugly added, "I won." This was not said with humor. It was said as a declaration of superiority deliberately designed to demean his former rival and *(kick him when he was down)*. Um…uh… Mr. President… *this is America; we don't do that…*

These comments did not come across well because they were mean spirited and unabashedly narcissistic. Although just these two comments have been isolated here, they more than adequately convey the attitude of superiority displayed by the President and his general demeanor during this entire meeting.

With just two sentences comprised of seven words, Barack Obama showed himself to be bereft of the social graces that would be expected of any normal person in such a setting; much less a president of the United States.

This display of ego, petulance and lack of decorum puts into question other issues of significantly more importance with regard to the measure of this man; who holds the highest office in the land and is the face of the United States to the world. Issues such as: Wisdom. Dignity. Maturity.

Afghanistan

President Barack Obama put off meeting with his top military commander in Afghanistan until October of 2009, a full six months after the new commander, General Stanley McCrystal, *(who Obama himself appointed)*, had taken command in the theater. And had the General not made public the fact that he had yet to meet with the President it is questionable as to whether this meeting would have been held that soon.

This meeting was quickly scheduled immediately after it became publicly known that President Obama had not yet met with his top theater commander.

It should be noted that General McCrystal did not disclose this information in an announcement of his own initiative, but rather, in answer to a question by a member of the press.

One would think that an ongoing war in which American troops were dying on a daily basis would give such a meeting a priority status. After all, Barack Obama had himself said that this was the war that America should be fighting: *instead of Iraq.*

It is difficult to determine if the delay in meeting with General McCrystal was due to Obama viewing Afghanistan as a low priority or not. But, the fact that the meeting was all of twenty-five minutes long and *squeezed* into the President's schedule because he was in Europe pitching Chicago as a host city to the International Olympic Committee… gives us a hint.

Ignoring the Republican Leadership

It was eight months before President Obama took the time to meet with the Republican leadership in Congress, and again, this belated meeting only took place after it became public knowledge that Obama had not yet held a meeting with the opposing party's congressional members. Once the news was out: a meeting was scheduled post haste.

Whether political adversaries or not, the Republican Party's elected officials represent nearly half of the country's voters and certainly should have been worthy of a meeting with a president: any president; particularly a new and inexperienced president.

These five instances certainly serve to raise serious questions as to this president's judgment. But they also raise questions about his level of knowledge, his ability to reason and his ability to act in an unbiased manner.

It is widely accepted that wisdom comes from maturity and maturity is acquired from experience: *that being life experience.*

In this president we see little of maturity and less yet of wisdom. Could it be that the academic cocoon in which this man was incubated provided little by the way of real life experience. Clearly it can be seen that whatever experience he was provided with has not prepared him for the station to which he has risen.

It is also evident that Barack Obama has not been tempered by disciplines that would cause him to exercise self-restraint, either.

Nor have fruits from the superior intellect Barack Obama is reputed to possess evidenced themselves in any recognizable manner.

What we do have is a man inbred with doctrines, who marches inexorably forward in his quest to impose these doctrines on the country with a complete abandon that is accompanied by an inexplicable disregard for the failures of the policies he has already initiated for their implementation.

So far at least, ignorance and arrogance seem to be prevailing on the part of the Obama administration and America seems to have elected a man whose ego far exceeds his ability. And if all of that was not bad enough, we now are starting to see the degree of arrogance and glaring absence of integrity possessed by Barack Obama.

At the time of this writing President Obama is trying to force religious institutions (namely Catholic hospitals and universities) to provide contraception and abortions for employees of those hospitals and universities.

Within the Affordable Care Act (the Health Care Bill) are provisions that specifically do not exempt these or other religious institutions from forced compliance to pay for insurance that must provide these benefits to women employed by these institutions.

Aside from being adverse to the tenets of the Christian faith, these provisions of this law also violate the separation of church and state clauses in the Constitution (the First Amendment).

When Barack Obama traveled throughout the United States in 2009 pushing his health care bill, he specifically, and without equivocation, stipulated repeatedly that his healthcare bill would not require taxpayers to pay for abortions and there would be no such provision in the new law.

We now know that this was a deception, to say the least. Unless we are to believe that *he also, did not even read his own health care bill.*

Instead, now, Barack Obama is forcing all insurance companies to provide this coverage in their policies and by default, forcing employers, no matter who they are, to pay for these services because the employers have to pay the bulk of the insurance premiums.

Washington insiders point out that this forced policy to provide all women with free contraception and abortions was an appeal to capture the majority of women's votes and that's why it is being pushed this year.

It is now very clear that there are no limits to this president's reach for power: even to usurp the Constitution of the United States to advance his ideological agenda. And, there are no limits to the tactics that he will use to deceive the American people, either.

The incidents and issues outlined in this chapter have concerned themselves with the arrogance, ignorance, petulance, incompetence and absence of integrity displayed by President Barack Obama. None of these things, however, can be considered to be definitively anti-American.

However, this is not so for many of the positions and policies of the Obama Administration, which have ranged from un-American to outright *anti-American* in their nature.

UN-AMERICAN
Exploits

VIII. UN-AMERICAN Exploits

Relative to issues that fall within the President's areas of responsibility Barack Obama has taken numerous positions that are extremely unpopular and widely viewed as un-American and, in some cases: just plain anti-American. Several of the controversial policies in question have to do with terrorism and national security.

The Obama Administration is of the view that the rights of United States citizens should be extended to enemy combatants and terrorists. The Administration takes this as far as to assert that enemy combatants should be given Miranda warnings (you have the right to remain silent, the right to an attorney, etc.) upon capture and *on the battlefield, no less!* And yes, these combatants would have court appointed lawyers – paid for by American taxpayers. It is most certainly anti-American to insist that Americans be forced to provide the defense for their enemies and then also be required to pay for that defense.

Then there is the Obama administration's absolutely ludicrous practice of deliberately not calling Islamic terrorists, Islamic terrorists. This of course, is done to avoid offending Muslims. If not anti-American, the policy is nothing short of ridiculous on its face. This

infantile denial of the obvious to protect groups or classes from being offended (and therefore discriminated against) should not be extended to people who want to destroy America and kill as many Americans as they can on top of the thousands they've already murdered. And… by the way…
to most Americans… this is offensive.

The Obama administration had even refused to concede that the Fort Hood massacre was a terrorist act, let alone an Islamic terrorist act. This is even after the facts came out verifying that the perpetrator, Nidal Malik Hasan, was indeed a Muslim intent on committing an act of terrorism against the United States.

As it turns out, there were numerous signs of Hasan's radicalization, but those who observed the changes in his behavior did not report them for fear of being accused of discriminating against Muslims and doing something that would be considered to be politically incorrect.

Janet Napolitano, Secretary of Homeland Security, (appointed by Barack Obama), refuses even to call terrorism, terrorism, instead calling acts of terrorism *man-made disasters* or *the acts of violent extremists.*

Napolitano is the one who said that the system was working (meaning the security procedures) when the underwear bomber was caught (by passengers) after the explosives packed in his underwear failed to explode and destroy the plane he was on as it was landing in Detroit. If Napolitano thinks that this result means that our security procedures were working we might as well all give up right now. To be blunt: the system didn't work – at all! Were it not for a clumsy, poorly trained terrorist, faulty explosives and a brave passenger there most assuredly would have been yet another catastrophic disaster in the United States. The Obama administration tried to relegate this incident to the act of a lone mal-content instead of correctly calling it what it was: an Islamic terrorist attack.

In truth America's security policies are seriously flawed because the policies in place to be politically correct are enforced more strongly than the country's anti-terrorism security policies. To be sure, a security official guilty of negligence would be dealt with less harshly than would one who was caught doing something that was considered to be politically incorrect.

Aside from being unintelligent to the point of being idiotic, it is most certainly anti-American to place the rights and sensibilities of terror suspects (because of their race or class or religion) above those of the citizens of the United States: especially when in so doing the government increases the risks to the American public by denying who its enemies really are, and then further increases those risks by lessening, and even prohibiting, security measures that can identify those who are most likely to be terrorists; *because such security measures as these would be politically incorrect.*

It is simply irrational to employ security measures that are unbiased. We know who the terrorists are. They fit a specific profile group. They are of specific nationalities. They are believers in a specific religion. Ignoring these FACTS is reckless and nothing short of inviting disaster. Time and again we have seen that providing protection for a class or group is more important to this administration than protecting the rights or safety of the majority of Americans.

Other Obama policies that can clearly be considered to be anti-American have to do with immigration and border security.

First is the failure of the Administration to build the fence on the southern border of the United States. The majority of Americans want the fence built and they are angry and resentful towards the government for not taking this simple measure. Everyone is aware that this is where the majority of the illegal aliens gain entry to the country. And it is not just a matter of immigration policy: it is also a safety and security issue. We are at war.

To be fair, this issue cannot just be laid at the feet of Barack Obama. The fence should have been built within a year of 911. But, President Bush didn't do it, the Republicans didn't do it and of course, the Democrats wouldn't do it.

The question is why? The most widely accepted beliefs are that the Republicans want the cheap labor that the illegal aliens provide and that the Democrats want the votes that the illegal aliens provide. The latter is correct and the former reason may be as well, but these are not the reasons that are given by the two political parties. Instead they argue that a fence won't work: This is in spite of the fact that the officials responsible for the security of Israel say theirs does; and the additional fact that it has also worked in southern California where it has been built near San Diego.

So, both parties are guilty of not complying with the will of the people and both are guilty of allowing a clear breach in the country's security.

But, Barack Obama bears the guilt now. As the newly elected President, having a clear majority in both houses of congress, and knowing fully the will of the American people, he could have built the fence without opposition. But he didn't. Instead he has stated that the borders are more secure than they have ever been, citing increased deportations of illegal aliens.

However, increased deportations don't necessarily translate to better border security. Increased deportations can also be an indicator of an increase in attempts to enter the country illegally.

Whether the number of illegal aliens entering the country has increased or not, they still number in the millions every year and present financial, health and security risks to the American people.

It is simply undeniable that the fence would provide additional, and much needed, security on the border. When fences have been employed, both in this country and abroad, they have had a dramatic effect on decreasing illegal entries. This is an indisputable fact.

Despite this empirical evidence, Obama still refuses to build the fence and sure up the country's border security. Whatever his reasons, they obviously do not serve America's best interests.

Barack Obama though, has taken things far beyond just failure to enforce the federal laws that pertain to illegal immigration. He has actually directed the Justice Department of the United States to mount a legal campaign against the State of Arizona *on behalf of the illegal immigrants* and file a lawsuit against the State to prevent it from enacting or enforcing its own immigration laws.

Arizona had enacted its own immigration laws because of the Obama Administration's refusal to enforce the federal laws or do anything to stem the tide of the increasing crime and violence being experienced by Arizona residents at the hands of the illegal aliens who were increasingly pouring into the state.

As justification for the lawsuit against the State of Arizona, Obama's Attorney General, Eric Holder, asserted that Arizona's law was discriminatory.

This announcement was made by Holder before he had even read the Arizona law.

Had he read it, he would have discovered that the new Arizona immigration laws were deliberately modeled after the existing federal immigration laws and were merely a reflection of them. If the Arizona laws were discriminatory, then so were those of the Federal Government.

The actions of the Obama Administration concerning the Arizona law amply illustrate that this president places the rights of non-citizens, and even illegal aliens who have gained entry to the country, above those of American citizens and, above even the sovereignty of one of the fifty United States.

And Barack Obama's anti-American policies don't stop at the country's borders. They extend to foreign policy too and are applied to our overseas allies. Obama has now failed to live up to America's pledge to support Israel (our long time ally in the middle-east). Instead he has withdrawn support for Israel and given it over to the Palestinians with whom the Israelis are negotiating over territory.

The United States has supported Israel since that nation's *re-creation* in 1948. Israel is our staunchest ally in the Middle East and it is the only ally we have in that entire region that has the courage of their convictions: Those being freedom and democracy.

The other states in the region, aside from Iraq whose fate is undetermined, are Muslim theocracies and for the most part, very anti-American.

Again, on the terrorism front, yet another of Obama's policies is demonstrative of his administration's anti-American postures. This being the administration's announcement that it was going to pursue the prosecution of CIA personnel for the interrogation techniques they used under the direction of the former administration (that of George W. Bush). This policy needs no mention as to why it is anti-American: only that it is astoundingly so.

And then, as if all of this wasn't enough, the Obama Administration caused outrage over its plans to put the terrorists responsible for the 911 attacks on trial: in New York City. Not just in the U.S. In New York City specifically.

These trials would certainly be tempting targets for additional terrorist attacks, but even if that were not so these plans showed an absolute disregard for, and ignorance of, the feelings of the American people with regard to 911. The 911 attacks were absolutely traumatic to the American people.

The Obama Administration's intention to hold these trials in this country in the very location where the terrorists committed the greatest of their massacres and the Administration's failure to recognize that this would present a problem for New Yorkers is absolutely stunning and tells us all something about Obama and the individuals he appointed to his administration.

It tells us that this event did not register with them as it did with the rest of us. It tells us that 911 doesn't hold the importance to them that it does to the rest of us.

The incognizance they displayed concerning the feelings of Americans about 911 evidences that the events of that day are not as significant to them as they are to the rest us.

Is disregard for the feelings of Americans about this event un-American? Absolutely it is! So much so that it is probably the most offensive of all the un-American things that this administration has been guilty of.

The feelings of most Americans towards 911 are that: this day... and these events... are sacred to us... They are sacrosanct.

Barack Obama *completely missed this.*

He missed it because he does not share those same feelings. He doesn't share those feelings because he doesn't have the same love of country as the rest of us.

Barack Hussein Obama doesn't view this day as sacred because he sees America as... *having little that is sacred.*

WHAT OBAMA'S
RE-ELECTION WILL MEAN

XI. What Obama's Re-Election Will Mean

Barack Obama has been very adept at disguising his true intentions since long before he was elected as president and he will continue to deceive the American public as to his real policies and intentions during this re-election campaign year. But, make no mistake: Barack Obama is a committed socialist and an *elitist* who thinks that his idea of government is better than that of most Americans.

His idea of government is absolutely antithetical to everything that America stands for and the opposite of the system of government that has made the United States the great country that it has become.

Barack Obama conducts himself as if he is a dictator because he believes that he is smarter than the founders of our country. He believes in class favoritism and he further believes that Marxist socialism, in which the government controls all facets of society and all commerce and industry (and therefore the purse strings), is better than the capitalist free enterprise society that is America.

The United States is a democratic-republic. It is not, nor was it ever intended to be, a pure democracy. In America the people elect representatives to work on their behalf when running the federal government. These representatives are consequently accountable to the Americans who have elected them.

Barack Obama does not believe in this system or accountability to the people. In a Marxist society the officials in power do what they wish to do, regardless of the wishes of the society's citizens. They do what they think is best: this is what Barack Obama believes in. This is why he conducts himself as if he is a dictator. This is why he scorns so much about America and why he is so radically indifferent to the country's constitution. He doesn't believe in it.

This is the truth about Barack Obama and every American needs to realize this and let it sink in because Obama will use his considerable public speaking talents and his **BILLION DOLLAR** war chest to persuade people that he is not the committed socialist that he actually is. And he and the Democratic Party Progressives will use every dirty trick (including voter fraud and intimidation, telling lies and mounting huge deceptive and untrue advertising campaigns) to get him re-elected.

There are no laws preventing parties or candidates from running ads that are untrue or deceptive and we can expect to see a deluge of this type of unethical campaigning from the Obama camp. This is what he did against Hillary Clinton and this type of negative "smear" campaigning will be stepped up during Obama's re-election campaign this year.

All Americans should be cautioned not to believe this man when he speaks. Even among his constituencies, Barack Obama is already notorious for stating one thing and doing another.

Americans should instead, look back at his record of policies and performance for the three years that he has been in office. What are his accomplishments? Many are cited in the previous chapters of this book.

The following is what we *should* expect from an Obama Administration should he be re-elected to the presidency.

BIGGER Government. Barack Obama's idea of government is that it is BIG. He has dramatically increased the size of the federal government in just his three years in office and he has given new and unprecedented powers to federal government agencies and unleashed them on both businesses (stifling them with over regulation and costs) and private citizens (e.g.: forcing citizens to pay for abortions irregardless of their beliefs on the subject).

These are just two examples of Obama's staunch advocacy for government overreach. If he is re-elected the size of the federal government *will increase dramatically*. The federal government *will be involved in your personal life*.

BIGGER DEFICITS. With bigger government will come even larger budget deficits. It can be no other way. America cannot pay for its huge government and the services that government provides right now. This is the reason for the country's ever increasing deficits – *not taxes being too low*. The United States is collecting more in taxes now than it ever has and yet the deficit continues to grow: *because of government overspending - not from government under-taxing*.

NO "FEASIBLE" ECONOMIC PLAN and Continued Unemployment. President Obama spent his entire first year in office giving his attention and time to the advancement of his plan for national health care while ignoring the economy, which had collapsed that year.

Since then he has launched a number of haphazard and ineffective plans to revive or stimulate the economy, the most notable of which was the so-called "Stimulus Plan", which failed in dramatic fashion due to the money *($800,000,000,000. - that's Eight Hundred Billion dollars of taxpayers' money)* being spent on things that would not stimulate the economy of any capitalist system.

Other than this, the bulk of the government funding has been given to Obama's pet *green initiatives,* the majority of which are based upon premature or faulty technologies and the majority of which, have failed, such as Solyndra, mentioned earlier in this book.

To date Obama has yet to put forward any economic plan that business leaders consider as sound or likely to stimulate the economy.

In fact, unbelievably, the Obama Administration is once again encouraging the practice of giving high-risk loans to minorities and having Fannie Mae and Freddie Mac guarantee them against failure (these are government loans backed with your money). This is in the face of the recent economic catastrophes that were the direct result of these Democratic Party policies to extend these risky loans in the first place.

The insanity of continuing practices that collapsed the economy in the first place is beyond reason and can only be attributed to Obama's rigid ideology.

Under the Obama Administration welfare, food stamps and other government aid programs are again increasing.

Beyond all of this, there aren't any individuals in the Obama Administration that have any practical experience in small business (small businesses are responsible for the majority of new jobs created in the U.S.).

Since his election, Barack Obama has resisted appointing individuals that have any private sector business experience to cabinet posts or to head any of the government agencies or departments that affect the economy, and instead, has continued to appoint bureaucrats or politicians to these positions. It is no wonder that his administration has been devoid of any sensible ideas to improve economic conditions in the country.

Obama's statements that his Administration has created 3 million jobs is unequivocally **untrue.** It is an audacious lie with no facts to support it.

The facts are: *that we have two million less employed people now than we did when Barack Obama assumed the office of the presidency.*

NO BORDER SECURITY or Immigration Policy.
President Obama has done little to secure America's borders. Rather, he has challenged the rights of states to protect their borders and citizens. Likewise, he has been more concerned with the rights of illegal aliens than those of American citizens.

Neither has he or the Democratic Party put forward any plan to remedy the faulty and unfair immigration policies of the United States or to mitigate the risks to security with regard to not just terrorism or drug trafficking presented by illegal aliens, but also the many serious diseases that are being re-introduced into American society (in and of themselves a risk to the health and security of the people of the United States).

The re-introduction of serious diseases to the U.S. is a subject that is *flying under the radar* right now, but it is happening: and in no small measure. Already we are seeing the spread of Tuberculosis and Polio (this disease had been eradicated completely in the United States) throughout the country.

As long as illegal aliens pour into the country along America's southwest borders these and other diseases will be re-introduced and spread to the American public.

The threat from infectious diseases is every bit as dangerous as that posed by terrorism. The risk of new pandemics from diseases against which the American public is no longer inoculated is quite real.

And no one is paying attention...

CLASS WARFARE and Racial Strife. The *class warfare* being instigated by Barack Obama bears with it implications of increased racial strife as well as tensions between the economic classes.

Unfortunately, in the United States, governmental aid and welfare programs are disproportionately (as a percent to the population) disbursed to minorities (the black and hispanic populations) of the country. If the fires of resentment between classes are stoked this could easily lead to heightened racial tensions, if for no other reason than that the lower income classes are so heavily populated by these minorities.

Insensitivity to the possibility of racial strife by such a staunch civil rights advocate is mystifying. Perhaps Obama is unaware of the demographics of the economic groups that he is trying to set against each other. Personally igniting resentment between the classes with zeal and without regard for the detrimental effects of the example he himself is setting is foolish and risky under any circumstances and again brings into question this president's astounding lack of judgment.

Based upon the poor judgment he showed concerning the Skip Gates incident and also that of his Administration's decision not to prosecute the Black Panthers in Philadelphia in a clear case of voter intimidation shows us that he is unconcerned about racial harmony and, he indeed, has done little if anything to improve relations between any classes in this country; racial or otherwise.

One would think that since Barack Obama is the first black president in the history of the country that he would use this fact to mitigate racial tensions. Unfortunately, by his actions and those of his administration, this president has set race relations back, if anything. Do not look for class or race relations to improve if Obama is re-elected. Look for them to worsen.

A WEAKER MILITARY and Dangerous Foreign Policies. Very few presidents have demonstrated the sheer ineptitude of President Barack Obama in terms of both military strategy and foreign policy. From his naïve position of announcing the withdrawal dates for

American military forces from theaters of war to his mishandling of virtually every situation in the Middle-East, he has demonstrated ineptitude that is astounding and nothing short of dangerous.

Obama proudly hails that he killed Osama Bin Laden. It is true that the capture and execution of this villainous murderer did happen on his watch, but there were a lot of intelligence assets and thousands of people employed in this manhunt before he took office and he had little to do with the event itself.

To give Obama his due, he can take credit for the increased use of unmanned drones to kill the enemy and destroy his assets. This has saved many American lives.

However, aside from this, Barack Obama has done little to make the world safer, and in fact, has employed strategies that will most certainly have the opposite effect, as in the case of his inaction concerning Iran when its population had risen up and had the momentum to unseat the Muslim extremists ruling that country. Millions of rioters in Tehran (the capital of Iran) chanted "Obama help us!" repeatedly as they protested against the Islamic extremists. Obama did nothing because he feared that if he acted on behalf of the protesters or spoke out it would hurt his possibilities to negotiate with the ruling faction of that country. He remained mute.

He did intervene in Libya militarily, but has done little to prevent Muslim extremists from taking power in that nation now that Khadafi is gone. And of course, they are.

The same can be said for Egypt, which now is in turmoil and in danger of being taken over by the "Muslim Brotherhood" (the progenitor of all Muslim extremist groups).

Obama optimistically assessed uprisings throughout the Mid-East (the "Arab Spring") as positive developments without giving consideration to the possibility that these transitions and power vacuums would present great opportunities for the Islamic extremists to seize power in these countries, which is in fact what has happened, which will, in turn, make the Middle-East an even more dangerous region.

President Obama simply does not have a good grasp on the history of this region, the countries involved, or Islam itself, to make sound assessments and therefore he is indecisive and invariably makes the wrong decisions when he does take a position.

Don't expect that to change. Barack Obama fancies himself to be a global leader, but he has little skill and has had almost no success in dealing with foreign leaders of any stripe. His missed opportunities concerning Iran have now put the entire world in jeopardy of nuclear exchanges as the fanatics in that country press on with their development of nuclear weapons, unabated.

Obama could have employed stronger sanctions against Iran, crippling their economy and ability to continue with their nuclear programs; but he didn't.

SYROCKETING ENERGY COSTS for American Businesses and Families. Gasoline prices have risen ninety percent (90%) since Barack Obama took office and this is far from the end of the increases. It is his intention to make these prices escalate much more dramatically to force the use of alternative fuels. He said this in his election campaign in 2008.

Gasoline prices affect the prices of all goods and commodities that we use: whether they are groceries, clothing, office supplies, or whatever; they have to be shipped so the increased fuel costs, in turn, increase the prices of everything else. The same effect is true for the escalating home heating fuels as well.

If Obama is re-elected Americans can expect much higher energy costs that will strain the budgets of families and businesses alike.

We are not talking about modest increases that are tolerable: we are looking at the same gas prices they are paying in the socialist European countries: *Five to six dollars a gallon for regular gasoline!*

That will be another 50% increase on top of what the price is now and this fifty percent increase will drastically affect the life style of every single American. And it won't stop there.

It was only the mid-term Congressional elections held in 2010, which gave control of the House of Representatives back to the Republican Party, that stopped President Obama and the Democrats from enacting the Cap 'N' Trade Bill, which would have taxed all forms of fossil fuels at inordinately high levels and sky-rocketed energy costs for every household and business in the United States. This would mean fifty to sixty per cent increases to the cost of all types of energy (electric, natural gas, coal, gasoline, oil and nuclear).

And, the Cap 'N' Trade Bill is far from dead. It will take only the re-election of Barack Obama and a handful of Democratic congresspersons to make it a reality and force it upon the American people. Then life will change for everyone... and not for the better.

An Obama re-election will undoubtedly bring about many, if not all, of these outcomes. It will because, as we have all seen, Obama is undeterred by the failures of his policies. He is a strident advocate for his ideology and his ideology is that of a socialist-elitist. He is not going to change.

If anything, a re-election will make him even more aggressive in his attempts to socialize America and transfer wealth from the people who earn incomes, to those who do not.

This is what an Obama re-election will bring about.

The 2012 election will be the most important in the lifetimes of most of us. We must all consider if we wish to again elect to the presidency a man who considers himself to be above the rest of us... and even *"Above America."*

To The Next

"American" President

To The Next "American" President

If you are elected to be the next President of the United States then, we the people, wish make to make an appeal... to you.

We the people of the United States of America appeal to you to truly be: an "American" President.

One, who not only believes in our Constitution, but enforces it, preserves it, and defends it: as your oath of office will call you to do.

One who, like Washington, imposes his virtue on the office, and imbues it with dignity.

One who, like Washington, doesn't forego integrity for the sake of approval, or the doctrines of party.

One who, like Lincoln, has the courage to do what is right... No Matter What The Cost.

We the people of America appeal to you to be a president who sees us as a whole; and not as classes or races; but as a whole people, for whom our Constitution was written. And we ask you to see each of us individually as the object of that Constitution: because as individual Americans; each of is.

We the people, ask you to hold sacred, the trust we place in you for the governance of our country, and the protection of it.

And, we the people, ask you to hold America sacred: because it is.

America can no longer afford political officials who use the powers entrusted in them to their own ends; or those of a party; or those of a class; or those of a race; or those of any other than the whole of us.

America can no longer afford officials in authority, elected or otherwise, who do their will, and not that of the people.

And...America can no longer afford a president who allows any of these to happen: even if tacitly.

If you are now elected to be the next President of the United States, you will then need to be... a president of the people, by the people, and for the people.

You will need to be so because... America needs you to be so.

The Constitution

The Constitution of The United States

We the People of the United States, in Order to form a more perfect Union, establish Justice, insure domestic Tranquility, provide for the common defence, promote the general Welfare, and secure the Blessings of Liberty to ourselves and our Posterity, do ordain and establish this Constitution for the United States of America.

Article 1.

Section 1

All legislative Powers herein granted shall be vested in a Congress of the United States, which shall consist of a Senate and House of Representatives.

Section 2

The House of Representatives shall be composed of Members chosen every second Year by the People of the several States, and the Electors in each State shall have the Qualifications requisite for Electors of the most numerous Branch of the State Legislature.

No Person shall be a Representative who shall not have attained to the Age of twenty five Years, and been seven Years a Citizen of the United States, and who shall not, when elected, be an Inhabitant of that State in which he shall be chosen.

Representatives and direct Taxes shall be apportioned among the several States which may be included within this Union, according to their respective Numbers, which shall be determined by adding to the whole Number of free Persons, including those bound to Service for a Term of Years, and excluding Indians not taxed, three fifths of all other Persons.

The actual Enumeration shall be made within three Years after the first Meeting of the Congress of the United States, and within every subsequent Term of ten Years, in such Manner as they shall by Law direct. The Number of Representatives shall not exceed one for every thirty Thousand, but each State shall have at Least one Representative; and until such enumeration shall be made, the State of New Hampshire shall be entitled to choose three, Massachusetts eight, Rhode Island and Providence Plantations one, Connecticut five, New York six, New Jersey four, Pennsylvania eight, Delaware one, Maryland six, Virginia ten, North Carolina five, South Carolina five and Georgia three. When vacancies happen in the Representation from any State, the Executive Authority thereof shall issue Writs of Election to fill such Vacancies.

The House of Representatives shall choose their Speaker and other Officers; and shall have the sole Power of Impeachment.

Section 3

The Senate of the United States shall be composed of two Senators from each State, chosen by the Legislature thereof, for six Years; and each Senator shall have one Vote.

Immediately after they shall be assembled in Consequence of the first Election, they shall be divided as equally as may be into three Classes. The Seats of the Senators of the first Class shall be vacated at the Expiration of the second Year, of the second Class at the Expiration of the fourth Year, and of the third Class at the Expiration of the sixth Year, so that one third may be chosen every second Year; and if Vacancies happen by Resignation, or otherwise, during the Recess of the Legislature of any State, the Executive thereof may make temporary Appointments until the next Meeting of the Legislature, which shall then fill such Vacancies.

No person shall be a Senator who shall not have attained to the Age of thirty Years, and been nine Years a Citizen of the United States, and who shall not, when elected, be an Inhabitant of that State for which he shall be chosen.

The Vice President of the United States shall be President of the Senate, but shall have no Vote, unless they be equally divided.

The Senate shall choose their other Officers, and also a President pro tempore, in the absence of the Vice President, or when he shall exercise the Office of President of the United States.

The Senate shall have the sole Power to try all Impeachments. When sitting for that Purpose, they shall be on Oath or Affirmation. When the President of the United States is tried, the Chief Justice shall preside: And no Person shall be convicted without the Concurrence of two thirds of the Members present.

Judgment in Cases of Impeachment shall not extend further than to removal from Office, and disqualification to hold and enjoy any Office of honor, Trust or Profit under the United States: but the Party convicted shall nevertheless be liable and subject to Indictment, Trial, Judgment and Punishment, according to Law.

Section 4
The Times, Places and Manner of holding Elections for Senators and Representatives, shall be prescribed in each State by the Legislature thereof; but the Congress may at any time by Law make or alter such Regulations, except as to the Place of Choosing Senators.

The Congress shall assemble at least once in every Year, and such Meeting shall be on the first Monday in December, unless they shall by Law appoint a different Day.

Section 5
Each House shall be the Judge of the Elections, Returns and Qualifications of its own Members, and a Majority of each shall constitute a Quorum to do Business; but a smaller number may adjourn from day to day, and may be authorized to compel the Attendance of absent Members, in such

Manner, and under such Penalties as each House may provide.

Each House may determine the Rules of its Proceedings, punish its Members for disorderly Behavior, and, with the Concurrence of two-thirds, expel a Member.

Each House shall keep a Journal of its Proceedings, and from time to time publish the same, excepting such Parts as may in their Judgment require Secrecy; and the Yeas and Nays of the Members of either House on any question shall, at the Desire of one fifth of those Present, be entered on the Journal.

Neither House, during the Session of Congress, shall, without the Consent of the other, adjourn for more than three days, nor to any other Place than that in which the two Houses shall be sitting.

Section 6

The Senators and Representatives shall receive a Compensation for their Services, to be ascertained by Law, and paid out of the Treasury of the United States. They shall in all Cases, except Treason, Felony and Breach of the Peace, be privileged from Arrest during their Attendance at the Session of their respective Houses, and in going to and returning from the same; and for any Speech or Debate in either House, they shall not be questioned in any other Place.

No Senator or Representative shall, during the Time for which he was elected, be appointed to any civil Office under the Authority of the United States which shall have been created, or the Emoluments whereof shall have been increased during such time; and no Person holding any Office under the United States, shall be a Member of either House during his Continuance in Office.

Section 7

All bills for raising Revenue shall originate in the House of Representatives; but the Senate may propose or concur with Amendments as on other Bills.

Every Bill which shall have passed the House of Representatives and the Senate, shall, before it become a Law, be presented to the President of the United States; If he approve he shall sign it, but if not he shall return it, with his Objections to that House in which it shall have originated, who shall enter the Objections at large on their Journal, and proceed to reconsider it. If after such Reconsideration two thirds of that House shall agree to pass the Bill, it shall be sent, together with the Objections, to the other House, by which it shall likewise be reconsidered, and if approved by two thirds of that House, it shall become a Law. But in all such Cases the Votes of both Houses shall be determined by Yeas and Nays, and the Names of the Persons voting for and against the Bill shall be entered on the Journal of each House respectively. If any Bill shall not be returned by the President within ten Days (Sundays excepted) after it shall have been presented to him, the Same shall be a *Law*, in like *Manner* as if he had signed it, unless the *Congress* by their *Adjournment* prevent its *Return*, in which *Case* it shall not be a *Law*.

Every *Order*, *Resolution*, or *Vote* to which the *Concurrence* of the *Senate* and *House* of *Representatives* may be necessary (except on a question of *Adjournment*) shall be presented to the *President* of the *United States*; and before the *Same* shall take *Effect*, shall be approved by him, or being disapproved by him, shall be repassed by two thirds of the *Senate* and *House* of *Representatives*, according to the *Rules* and *Limitations* prescribed in the *Case* of a *Bill*.

Section 8

The *Congress* shall have *Power* *To* lay and collect *Taxes*, *Duties*, *Imposts* and *Excises*, to pay the *Debts* and provide for the common *Defence* and general *Welfare* of the *United States*; but all *Duties*, *Imposts* and *Excises* shall be uniform throughout the United States; To borrow money on the credit of the United States;

To regulate Commerce with foreign Nations, and among the several States, and with the Indian Tribes; To establish an uniform Rule of Naturalization, and uniform Laws on the subject of Bankruptcies throughout the United States;

To coin Money, regulate the Value thereof, and of foreign Coin, and fix the Standard of Weights and Measures;

To provide for the Punishment of counterfeiting the Securities and current Coin of the United States;

To establish Post Offices and Post Roads;

To promote the Progress of Science and useful Arts, by securing for limited Times to Authors and Inventors the exclusive Right to their respective Writings and Discoveries;

To constitute Tribunals inferior to the supreme Court;

To define and punish Piracies and Felonies committed on the high Seas, and Offenses against the Law of Nations;

To declare War, grant Letters of Marque and Reprisal, and make Rules concerning Captures on Land and Water;

To raise and support Armies, but no Appropriation of Money to that Use shall be for a longer Term than two Years;

To provide and maintain a Navy;

To make Rules for the Government and Regulation of the land and naval Forces;

To provide for calling forth the Militia to execute the Laws of the Union, suppress Insurrections and repel Invasions;

To provide for organizing, arming, and disciplining, the Militia, and for governing such Part of them as may be employed in the Service of the United States, reserving to the States respectively, the Appointment of the Officers, and the Authority of training the Militia according to the discipline prescribed by Congress;

To exercise exclusive Legislation in all Cases whatsoever, over such District (not exceeding ten Miles square) as may, by Cession of particular States, and the acceptance of Congress, become the Seat of the Government of the United States, and to exercise like Authority over all Places purchased by the Consent of the Legislature of the State in which the Same shall be, for the Erection of Forts, Magazines, Arsenals, dock-Yards, and other needful Buildings; And To make all Laws which shall be necessary and proper for carrying into Execution the foregoing Powers, and all other Powers vested by this Constitution in the Government of the United States, or in any Department or Officer thereof.

Section 9

The Migration or Importation of such Persons as any of the States now existing shall think proper to admit, shall not be prohibited by the Congress prior to the Year one thousand eight hundred and eight, but a tax or duty may be imposed on such Importation, not exceeding ten dollars for each Person.

The privilege of the Writ of Habeas Corpus shall not be suspended, unless when in Cases of Rebellion or Invasion the public Safety may require it.

No Bill of Attainder or ex post facto Law shall be passed.

No capitation, or other direct, Tax shall be laid, unless in Proportion to the Census or Enumeration herein before directed to be taken.

No Tax or Duty shall be laid on Articles exported from any State.

No Preference shall be given by any Regulation of Commerce or Revenue to the Ports of one State over those of another: nor shall Vessels bound to, or from, one State, be obliged to enter, clear, or pay Duties in another.

No Money shall be drawn from the Treasury, but in Consequence of Appropriations made by Law; and a regular Statement and Account of the Receipts and Expenditures of all public Money shall be published from time to time.

No Title of Nobility shall be granted by the United States: And no Person holding any Office of Profit or Trust under them, shall, without the Consent of the Congress, accept of any present, Emolument, Office, or Title, of any kind whatever, from any King, Prince or foreign State.

Section 10
No State shall enter into any Treaty, Alliance, or Confederation; grant Letters of Marque and Reprisal; coin Money; emit Bills of Credit; make any Thing but

gold and silver Coin a Tender in Payment of Debts; pass any Bill of Attainder, ex post facto Law, or Law impairing the Obligation of Contracts, or grant any Title of Nobility.

No State shall, without the Consent of the Congress, lay any Imposts or Duties on Imports or Exports, except what may be absolutely necessary for executing its inspection Laws: and the net Produce of all Duties and Imposts, laid by any State on Imports or Exports, shall be for the Use of the Treasury of the United States; and all such Laws shall be subject to the Revision and Control of the Congress.

No State shall, without the Consent of Congress, lay any duty of Tonnage, keep Troops, or Ships of War in time of Peace, enter into any Agreement or Compact with another State, or with a foreign Power, or engage in War, unless actually invaded, or in such imminent Danger as will not admit of delay.

Article 2.

Section 1

The executive Power shall be vested in a President of the United States of America. He shall hold his Office during the Term of four Years, and, together with the Vice-President chosen for the same Term, be elected, as follows:

Each State shall appoint, in such Manner as the Legislature thereof may direct, a Number of Electors, equal to the whole Number of Senators and Representatives to which the State may be entitled in the Congress: but no Senator or Representative, or Person holding an Office of Trust or Profit under the United States, shall be appointed an Elector.

The Electors shall meet in their respective States, and vote by Ballot for two persons, of whom one at least shall not lie an Inhabitant of the same State with themselves. And they shall make a List of all the Persons voted for, and of the Number of Votes for each; which List they shall sign and certify, and transmit sealed to the Seat of the Government of the United States, directed to the President of the Senate. The President of the Senate shall, in the Presence of the Senate and House of Representatives, open all the Certificates, and the Votes shall then be counted. The Person having the greatest Number of Votes shall be the President, if such Number be a Majority of the whole Number of Electors appointed; and if there be more than one who have such Majority, and have an equal Number of Votes, then the House of Representatives shall immediately choose by Ballot one of them for President; and if no Person have a Majority, then from the five highest on the List the said House shall in like Manner choose the President. But in choosing the President, the Votes shall be taken by States, the Representation from each State having one Vote; a quorum for this Purpose shall consist of a Member or Members from two-thirds of the States, and a Majority of all the States shall be necessary to a Choice. In every Case, after the Choice of the President, the Person having the greatest Number of Votes of the Electors shall be the Vice President. But if there should remain two or more who have equal Votes, the Senate shall choose from them by Ballot the Vice-President.

The Congress may determine the Time of choosing the Electors, and the Day on which they shall give their Votes; which Day shall be the same throughout the United States.

No person except a natural born Citizen, or a Citizen of the United States, at the time of the Adoption of this Constitution, shall be eligible to the Office of President; neither shall any Person be eligible to that Office who shall not have attained to the Age of thirty-five Years, and been fourteen Years a Resident within the United States.

In Case of the Removal of the President from Office, or of his Death, Resignation, or Inability to discharge the Powers and Duties of the said Office, the same shall devolve on the Vice President, and the Congress may by Law provide for the Case of Removal, Death, Resignation or Inability, both of the President and Vice President, declaring what Officer shall then act as President, and such

Officer shall act accordingly, until the Disability be removed, or a President shall be elected.

The President shall, at stated Times, receive for his Services, a Compensation, which shall neither be increased nor diminished during the Period for which he shall have been elected, and he shall not receive within that Period any other Emolument from the United States, or any of them.

Before he enter on the Execution of his Office, he shall take the following Oath or Affirmation:

"I do solemnly swear (or affirm) that I will faithfully execute the Office of President of the United States, and will to the best of my Ability, preserve, protect and defend the Constitution of the United States."

Section 2
The President shall be Commander in Chief of the Army and Navy of the United States, and of the Militia of the several States, when called into the actual

Service of the United States; he may require the Opinion, in writing, of the principal Officer in each of the executive Departments, upon any subject relating to the Duties of their respective Offices, and he shall have Power to Grant Reprieves and Pardons for Offenses against the United States, except in Cases of Impeachment.

He shall have Power, by and with the Advice and Consent of the Senate, to make Treaties, provided two thirds of the Senators present concur; and he shall nominate, and by and with the Advice and Consent of the Senate, shall appoint Ambassadors, other public Ministers and Consuls, Judges of the supreme Court, and all other Officers of the United States, whose Appointments are not herein otherwise provided for, and which shall be established by Law: but the Congress may by Law vest the Appointment of such inferior Officers, as they think proper, in the President alone, in the Courts of Law, or in the Heads of Departments.

The President shall have Power to fill up all Vacancies that may happen during the Recess of the Senate, by granting

Commissions which shall expire at the End of their next Session.

Section 3

He shall from time to time give to the Congress Information of the State of the Union, and recommend to their Consideration such Measures as he shall judge necessary and expedient; he may, on extraordinary Occasions, convene both Houses, or either of them, and in Case of Disagreement between them, with Respect to the Time of Adjournment, he may adjourn them to such Time as he shall think proper; he shall receive Ambassadors and other public Ministers; he shall take Care that the Laws be faithfully executed, and shall Commission all the Officers of the United States.

Section 4

The President, Vice President and all civil Officers of the United States, shall be removed from Office on Impeachment for, and Conviction of, Treason, Bribery, or other high Crimes and Misdemeanors.

Article 3.

Section 1

The judicial Power of the United States, shall be vested in one supreme Court, and in such inferior Courts as the Congress may from time to time ordain and establish. The Judges, both of the supreme and inferior Courts, shall hold their Offices during good Behavior, and shall, at stated Times, receive for their Services a Compensation which shall not be diminished during their Continuance in Office.

Section 2

The judicial Power shall extend to all Cases, in Law and Equity, arising under this Constitution, the Laws of the United States, and Treaties made, or which shall be made, under their Authority; to all Cases affecting Ambassadors, other public Ministers and Consuls; to all Cases of admiralty and maritime Jurisdiction; to Controversies to which the United States shall be a Party; to Controversies between two or more States; between a State and Citizens of another State; between Citizens of different States; between

Citizens of the same State claiming Lands under Grants of different States, and between a State, or the Citizens thereof, and foreign States, Citizens or Subjects.

In all Cases affecting Ambassadors, other public Ministers and Consuls, and those in which a State shall be Party, the supreme Court shall have original Jurisdiction. In all the other Cases before mentioned, the supreme Court shall have appellate Jurisdiction, both as to Law and Fact, with such Exceptions, and under such Regulations as the Congress shall make.

The Trial of all Crimes, except in Cases of Impeachment, shall be by Jury; and such Trial shall be held in the State where the said Crimes shall have been committed; but when not committed within any State, the Trial shall be at such Place or Places as the Congress may by Law have directed.

Section 3

Treason against the United States, shall consist only in levying War against them, or in adhering to their Enemies, giving them Aid and Comfort. No Person shall be convicted of Treason unless on the Testimony of two Witnesses to the same overt Act, or on Confession in open Court.

The Congress shall have power to declare the Punishment of Treason, but no Attainder of Treason shall work Corruption of Blood, or Forfeiture except during the Life of the Person attainted.

Article 4.

Section 1

Full Faith and Credit shall be given in each State to the public Acts, Records, and judicial Proceedings of every other State. And the Congress may by general Laws prescribe the Manner in which such Acts, Records and Proceedings shall be proved, and the Effect thereof.

Section 2

The Citizens of each State shall be entitled to all Privileges and Immunities of Citizens in the several States.

A Person charged in any State with Treason, Felony, or other Crime, who shall flee from Justice, and be found in another State, shall on demand of the executive Authority of the State from which he fled, be delivered up, to be removed to the State having Jurisdiction of the Crime.

No Person held to Service or Labour in one State, under the Laws thereof, escaping into another, shall, in Consequence of any Law or Regulation therein, be discharged from such Service or Labour, But shall be delivered up on Claim of the Party to whom such Service or Labour may be due.

Section 3

New States may be admitted by the Congress into this Union; but no new States shall be formed or erected within the Jurisdiction of any other State; nor any State be formed by the Junction of two or more States, or parts of States, without the Consent of the Legislatures of the States concerned as well as of the Congress.

The Congress shall have Power to dispose of and make all needful Rules and Regulations respecting the Territory or other Property belonging to the United States; and nothing in this Constitution shall be so construed as to Prejudice any Claims of the United States, or of any particular State.

Section 4
The United States shall guarantee to every State in this Union a Republican Form of Government, and shall protect each of them against Invasion; and on Application of the Legislature, or of the Executive (when the Legislature cannot be convened) against domestic Violence.

Article 5.
The Congress, whenever two thirds of both Houses shall deem it necessary, shall propose Amendments to this Constitution, or, on the Application of the

Legislatures of two thirds of the several States, shall call a Convention for proposing Amendments, which, in either Case, shall be valid to all Intents and Purposes, as part of this Constitution, when ratified by the Legislatures of three fourths of the several States, or by Conventions in three fourths thereof, as the one or the other Mode of Ratification may be proposed by the Congress; Provided that no Amendment which may be made prior to the Year One thousand eight hundred and eight shall in any Manner affect the first and fourth Clauses in the Ninth Section of the first Article; and that no State, without its Consent, shall be deprived of its equal Suffrage in the Senate.

Article 6.

All Debts contracted and Engagements entered into, before the Adoption of this Constitution, shall be as valid against the United States under this Constitution, as under the Confederation.

This Constitution, and the Laws of the United States which shall be made in Pursuance thereof; and all Treaties made, or which shall be made, under the Authority of the United States, shall be the supreme Law of the Land; and the Judges in every State shall be bound thereby, any Thing in the Constitution or Laws of any State to the Contrary notwithstanding.

The Senators and Representatives before mentioned, and the Members of the several State Legislatures, and all executive and judicial Officers, both of the United States and of the several States, shall be bound by Oath or Affirmation, to support this Constitution; but no religious Test shall ever be required as a Qualification to any Office or public Trust under the United States.

Article 7.
The Ratification of the Conventions of nine States, shall be sufficient for the Establishment of this Constitution between the States so ratifying the Same.

Done in Convention by the Unanimous Consent of the States present the Seventeenth Day of September in the Year of our Lord one thousand seven hundred and Eighty seven and of the Independence of the United States of America the Twelfth. In Witness whereof We have hereunto subscribed our Names.

George Washington - President and deputy from Virginia

New Hampshire - John Langdon, Nicholas Gilman

Massachusetts - Nathaniel Gorham, Rufus King

Connecticut - William Samuel Johnson, Roger Sherman

New York - Alexander Hamilton

New Jersey - William Livingston, David Brearley, William Paterson, Jonathan Dayton

Pennsylvania - Benjamin Franklin, Thomas Mifflin, Robert Morris, George Clymer, Thomas Fitzsimons, Jared Ingersoll, James Wilson, Gouvernour Morris

Delaware - George Read, Gunning Bedford Jr., John Dickinson, Richard Bassett, Jacob Broom

Maryland - James McHenry, Daniel of St Thomas Jenifer, Daniel Carroll

Virginia - John Blair, James Madison Jr.

North Carolina - William Blount, Richard Dobbs Spaight, Hugh Williamson

South Carolina - John Rutledge, Charles Cotesworth Pinckney, Charles Pinckney, Pierce Butler

Georgia - William Few, Abraham Baldwin

Attest: William Jackson, Secretary

Amendment 1

Congress shall make no law respecting an establishment of religion, or prohibiting the free exercise thereof; or abridging the freedom of speech, or of the press; or the right of the people peaceably to assemble, and to petition the Government for a redress of grievances.

Amendment 2

A well regulated Militia, being necessary to the security of a free State, the right of the people to keep and bear Arms, shall not be infringed.

Amendment 3

No Soldier shall, in time of peace be quartered in any house, without the consent of the Owner, nor in time of war, but in a manner to be prescribed by law.

Amendment 4

The right of the people to be secure in their persons, houses, papers, and effects, against unreasonable searches and seizures, shall not be violated, and no Warrants shall issue, but upon probable cause, supported by Oath or affirmation, and particularly describing the place to be searched, and the persons or things to be seized.

Amendment 5

No person shall be held to answer for a capital, or otherwise infamous crime, unless on a presentment or indictment of a Grand Jury, except in cases arising in the land or naval forces, or in the Militia, when in actual service in time of War or public danger; nor shall any person be subject for the same offense to be twice put in jeopardy of life or limb; nor shall be compelled in any criminal case to be a witness against himself, nor be deprived of life, liberty, or property, without due process of law; nor shall private property be taken for public use, without just compensation.

Amendment 6

In all criminal prosecutions, the accused shall enjoy the right to a speedy and public trial, by an impartial jury of the State and district wherein the crime shall have been committed, which district shall have been previously ascertained by law, and to be informed of the nature and cause of the accusation; to be confronted with the witnesses against him; to have compulsory process for obtaining witnesses in his favor, and to have the Assistance of Counsel for his defence.

Amendment 7

In Suits at common law, where the value in controversy shall exceed twenty dollars, the right of trial by jury shall be preserved, and no fact tried by a jury, shall be otherwise re-examined in any Court of the United States, than according to the rules of the common law.

Amendment 8

Excessive bail shall not be required, nor excessive fines imposed, nor cruel and unusual punishments inflicted.

Amendment 9

The enumeration in the Constitution, of certain rights, shall not be construed to deny or disparage others retained by the people.

Amendment 10

The powers not delegated to the United States by the Constitution, nor prohibited by it to the States, are reserved to the States respectively, or to the people.

Amendment 11

The Judicial power of the United States shall not be construed to extend to any suit in law or equity, commenced or prosecuted against one of the United States by Citizens of another State, or by Citizens or Subjects of any Foreign State.

Amendment 12

The Electors shall meet in their respective states, and vote by ballot for President and Vice-President, one of whom, at least, shall not be an inhabitant of the same state with themselves; they shall name in their ballots the person voted for as President, and in distinct ballots the person voted for as Vice-President, and they shall make distinct lists of all persons voted for as President, and of all persons voted for as Vice-President and of the number of votes for each, which lists they shall sign and certify, and transmit sealed to the seat of the government of the United States, directed to the President of the Senate;

The President of the Senate shall, in the presence of the Senate and House of Representatives, open all the certificates and the votes shall then be counted;

The person having the greatest Number of votes for President, shall be the President, if such number be a majority of the whole number of Electors appointed; and if no person have such majority, then from the persons having the highest numbers not exceeding three on the list of those voted for as President, the House of Representatives shall choose immediately, by ballot, the President. But in choosing the President, the votes shall be taken by states, the representation from each state having one vote; a quorum for this purpose shall consist of a member or members from two-thirds of the states, and a majority of all the states shall be necessary to a choice. And if the House of Representatives shall not choose a President whenever the right of choice shall devolve upon them, before the fourth day of March next following, then the Vice-President shall act as President, as in the case of the death or other constitutional disability of the President.

The person having the greatest number of votes as Vice-President, shall be the Vice-President, if such number be a majority of the whole number of Electors appointed, and if no person have a majority, then from the two highest numbers on the list, the Senate shall choose the Vice-President; a quorum for the purpose shall consist of two-thirds of the whole number of Senators, and a majority of the whole number shall be necessary to a choice. But no person constitutionally ineligible to the office of President shall be eligible to that of Vice-President of the United States.

Amendment 13

1. Neither slavery nor involuntary servitude, except as a punishment for crime whereof the party shall have been duly convicted, shall exist within the United States, or any place subject to their jurisdiction.

2. Congress shall have power to enforce this article by appropriate legislation.

Amendment 14

1. All persons born or naturalized in the United States, and subject to the jurisdiction thereof, are citizens of the United States and of the State wherein they reside. No State shall make or enforce any law which shall abridge the privileges or immunities of citizens of the United States; nor shall any State deprive any person of life, liberty, or property, without due process of law; nor deny to any person within its jurisdiction the equal protection of the laws.

2. Representatives shall be apportioned among the several States according to their respective numbers, counting the

whole number of persons in each State, excluding Indians not taxed. But when the right to vote at any election for the choice of electors for President and Vice-President of the United States, Representatives in Congress, the Executive and Judicial officers of a State, or the members of the Legislature thereof, is denied to any of the male inhabitants of such State, being twenty-one years of age, and citizens of the United States, or in any way abridged, except for participation in rebellion, or other crime, the basis of representation therein shall be reduced in the proportion which the number of such male citizens shall bear to the whole number of male citizens twenty-one years of age in such State.

3. No person shall be a Senator or Representative in Congress, or elector of President and Vice-President, or hold any office, civil or military, under the United States, or under any State, who, having previously taken an oath, as a member of Congress, or as an officer of the United States, or as a member of any State legislature, or as an executive or judicial officer of any State, to support the Constitution of the United States, shall have engaged in insurrection or

rebellion against the same, or given aid or comfort to the enemies thereof. But Congress may by a vote of two-thirds of each House, remove such disability.

4. The validity of the public debt of the United States, authorized by law, including debts incurred for payment of pensions and bounties for services in suppressing insurrection or rebellion, shall not be questioned. But neither the United States nor any State shall assume or pay any debt or obligation incurred in aid of insurrection or rebellion against the United States, or any claim for the loss or emancipation of any slave; but all such debts, obligations and claims shall be held illegal and void.

5. The Congress shall have power to enforce, by appropriate legislation, the provisions of this article.

Amendment 15
1. The right of citizens of the United States to vote shall not be denied or abridged by the United States or by any State on account of race, color, or previous condition of servitude.

2. The Congress shall have power to enforce this article by appropriate legislation.

Amendment 16
The Congress shall have power to lay and collect taxes on incomes, from whatever source derived, without apportionment among the several States, and without regard to any census or enumeration.

Amendment 17
The Senate of the United States shall be composed of two Senators from each State, elected by the people thereof, for six years; and each Senator shall have one vote. The electors in each State shall have the qualifications requisite for electors of the most numerous branch of the State legislatures.

When vacancies happen in the representation of any State in the Senate, the executive authority of such State shall issue writs of election to fill such vacancies: Provided, That the legislature of any State may empower the executive thereof to make temporary appointments until the people fill the vacancies by election as the legislature may direct.

This amendment shall not be so construed as to affect the election or term of any Senator chosen before it becomes valid as part of the Constitution.

Amendment 18

1. After one year from the ratification of this article the manufacture, sale, or transportation of intoxicating liquors within, the importation thereof into, or the exportation thereof from the United States and all territory subject to the jurisdiction thereof for beverage purposes is hereby prohibited.

2. The Congress and the several States shall have concurrent power to enforce this article by appropriate legislation.

3. This article shall be inoperative unless it shall have been ratified as an amendment to the Constitution by the legislatures of the several States, as provided in the

Constitution, within seven years from the date of the submission hereof to the States by the Congress.

Amendment 19
The right of citizens of the United States to vote shall not be denied or abridged by the United States or by any State on account of sex.

Congress shall have power to enforce this article by appropriate legislation.

Amendment 20
1. The terms of the President and Vice President shall end at noon on the 20th day of January, and the terms of Senators and Representatives at noon on the 3d day of January, of the years in which such terms would have ended if this article had not been ratified; and the terms of their successors shall then begin.

2. The Congress shall assemble at least once in every year, and such meeting shall begin at noon on the 3d day of January, unless they shall by law appoint a different day.

3. If, at the time fixed for the beginning of the term of the President, the President elect shall have died, the Vice President elect shall become President. If a President shall not have been chosen before the time fixed for the beginning of his term, or if the President elect shall have failed to qualify, then the Vice President elect shall act as President until a President shall have qualified; and the Congress may by law provide for the case wherein neither a President elect nor a Vice President elect shall have qualified, declaring who shall then act as President, or the manner in which one who is to act shall be selected, and such person shall act accordingly until a President or Vice President shall have qualified.

4. The Congress may by law provide for the case of the death of any of the persons from whom the House of Representatives may choose a President whenever the right of choice shall have devolved upon them, and for the case of the death of any of the

persons from whom the Senate may choose a Vice President whenever the right of choice shall have devolved upon them.

5. Sections 1 and 2 shall take effect on the 15th day of October following the ratification of this article.

6. This article shall be inoperative unless it shall have been ratified as an amendment to the Constitution by the legislatures of three-fourths of the several States within seven years from the date of its submission.

Amendment 21
1. The eighteenth article of amendment to the Constitution of the United States is hereby repealed.

2. The transportation or importation into any State, Territory, or possession of the United States for delivery or use therein of intoxicating liquors, inviolation of the laws thereof, is hereby prohibited.

3. The article shall be inoperative unless it shall have been ratified as an amendment to the Constitution by conventions in the several States, as provided in the Constitution, within seven years from the date of the submission hereof to the States by the Congress.

Amendment 22

1. No person shall be elected to the office of the President more than twice, and no person who has held the office of President, or acted as President, for more than two years of a term to which some other person was elected President shall be elected to the office of the President more than once. But this Article shall not apply to any person holding the office of President, when this Article was proposed by the Congress, and shall not prevent any person who may be holding the office of President, or acting as President, during the term within which this Article becomes operative from holding the office of President or acting as President during the remainder of such term.

2. This article shall be inoperative unless it shall have been ratified as an amendment to the Constitution by the legislatures of three-fourths of the several States within seven years from the date of its submission to the States by the Congress.

Amendment 23

1. The District constituting the seat of Government of the United States shall appoint in such manner as the Congress may direct: A number of electors of President and Vice President equal to the whole number of Senators and Representatives in Congress to which the District would be entitled if it were a State, but in no event more than the least populous State; they shall be in addition to those appointed by the States, but they shall be considered, for the purposes of the election of President and Vice President, to be electors appointed by a State; and they shall meet in the District and perform such duties as provided by the twelfth article of amendment.

2. The Congress shall have power to enforce this article by appropriate legislation.

Amendment 24

1. The right of citizens of the United States to vote in any primary or other election for President or Vice President, for electors for President or Vice President, or for Senator or Representative in Congress, shall not be denied or abridged by the United States or any State by reason of failure to pay any poll tax or other tax.

2. The Congress shall have power to enforce this article by appropriate legislation.

Amendment 25

1. In case of the removal of the President from office or of his death or resignation, the Vice President shall become President.

2. Whenever there is a vacancy in the office of the Vice President, the President shall nominate a Vice President who shall take office upon confirmation by a majority vote of both Houses of Congress.

3. Whenever the President transmits to the President pro tempore of the Senate and the Speaker of the House of Representatives his written declaration that he is unable to discharge the powers and duties of his office, and until he transmits to them a written declaration to the contrary, such powers and duties shall be discharged by the Vice President as Acting President.

4. Whenever the Vice President and a majority of either the principal officers of the executive departments or of such other body as Congress may by law provide, transmit to the President pro tempore of the Senate and the Speaker of the House of Representatives their written declaration that the President is unable to discharge the powers and duties of his office, the Vice President shall immediately assume the powers and duties of the office as Acting President.

Thereafter, when the President transmits to the President pro tempore of the Senate and the Speaker of the House of Representatives his written declaration that no inability exists, he shall resume the powers and duties of his office unless the Vice President and a majority of either the principal officers of the executive department or of such other body as Congress may by law provide, transmit within four days to the President pro tempore of the Senate and the Speaker of the House of Representatives their written declaration that the President is unable to discharge the powers and duties of his office. Thereupon Congress shall decide the issue, assembling within forty eight hours for that purpose if not in session. If the Congress, within twenty one days after receipt of the latter written declaration, or, if Congress is not in session, within twenty one days after Congress is required to assemble, determines by two thirds vote of both Houses that the President is unable to discharge the powers and duties of his office, the Vice President shall continue to discharge the same as Acting President; otherwise, the President shall resume the powers and duties of his office.

Amendment 26

1. The right of citizens of the United States, who are eighteen years of age or older, to vote shall not be denied or abridged by the United States or by any State on account of age.

2. The Congress shall have power to enforce this article by appropriate legislation.

Amendment 27

No law, varying the compensation for the services of the Senators and Representatives, shall take effect, until an election of Representatives shall have intervened.

The Pledge of Allegiance

I pledge allegiance to the flag of the United States of America, and to the republic for which it stands, one nation, under God, indivisible, with liberty and justice for all.

The Pledge of Allegiance
As changed by the Executive Order
of Barack Obama on April 20, 2010

I pledge allegiance to the flag of the United States of America, and to the republic for which it stands, one nation, indivisible, with liberty and justice for all.

Definitions (extracted Merriam Webster Dictionary)

Progressives - The term *progressivism* emerged in reference to a more general response to the vast changes brought by industrialization: an alternative to the traditional conservative response to social and economic issues. Associated with left wing politics and the various streams of socialism or communism. The Progressive Party organized at the start of the 20th century, and progressivism made great strides under American presidents Theodore Roosevelt, Woodrow Wilson, Franklin Roosevelt and Lyndon Johnson.

Liberalism - a political philosophy based on belief in progress, the essential goodness of the human race, and the autonomy of the individual and standing for the protection of political and civil liberties; *specifically* : such a philosophy that considers government as a crucial instrument for amelioration of social inequities (as those involving race, gender, or class).

Leftists – Advocates of leftist political and economic philosophies such as progressivism, socialism and communism.

Sources:

The Constitution of the United States

New York Times

Boston Globe

pearsonschool.org

CNN

"Green Jobs: Help Wanted" Brett Baier, Fox News Channel

abcnews.go.com

usatoday.com

whitehouse.gov

online.wsj.com

foxnews.com

forbes.com

cnn.com

energytomorrow.org

bloomberg.com

washingtonexaminer.com

nationalreview.com

youtube.com

nationofchange.org

charlestoncitypaper.com

politico.com

pbs.org

dailycaller.com

newsmax.com